Judy Jacobs has paid a far greater price than the cost of this book for the revelation she shares. Reading it will enrich you and bring power to your faith.

—BISHOP T. D. JAKES SR.
THE POTTER'S HOUSE OF DALLAS, INC.

Judy Jacobs has a passion to see the body of Christ fully possess God's promises. *Take It by Force!* will challenge you to step out and believe for something more than you've seen while equipping you with practical tools to connect you with heaven's provision while here on earth.

—JOHN AND LISA BEVERE
AUTHORS/SPEAKERS
MESSENGER INTERNATIONAL

This anointed and timely book, *Take It by Force!*, can be your tool to plan your strategy to win and be victorious in every area of your life. As you read it, may you be filled with passion, zeal, and courage to become a believer of such violent faith that God can use to advance His kingdom and propel you into your destiny.

—BISHOP EDDIE L. LONG, SENIOR PASTOR
NEW BIRTH MISSIONARY BAPTIST CHURCH

This book is right on time! *Take It by Force!* brings home the importance of seeking God relentlessly in pursuit of His promises. In this book, Judy reminds us that many of the answers we seek can only be found in the deepest form of obedience— inexplicable, unyielding, crazy faith. It is there that your miracle lies in wait, *"…and the violent take it by force."*

—PAULA WHITE
BEST-SELLING AUTHOR AND SPEAKER
CO-PASTOR, WITHOUT WALLS INTERNATIONAL CHURCH

It gives me great pleasure to recommend Judy Jacobs-Tuttle's book, *Take It by Force!* In a time when compromise, carelessness, and complacency have replaced conviction, concern, and character, Judy shoots straight and hits the mark, urging and admonishing the church to reach for its God-given potential.

I believe we are seeing a generation of believers who are no longer content mired in the marshlands of mediocrity, but who will only be satisfied when their feet are on paths leading them to higher ground.

There are victories to be won, vistas to be seen, and adversaries to be defeated for the glory of God and in the name of His Christ. Judy Jacobs-Tuttle is sending a clear message to all who will receive it—you don't have to be satisfied where you are; you can take what rightfully belongs to you with violent faith!

—PASTOR ROD PARSLEY
AUTHOR, *SILENT NO MORE*
PASTOR, WORLD HARVEST CHURCH

This book is a mandate for every believer who recognizes his or her destiny moment. On the pages of this book are God-breathed words that will stir and commission you to take this kingdom by force. It is time for the saints to possess the kingdom. Hear the wake-up call of an impassioned writer who lives what she writes. Judy Jacobs is a passionate woman who is sounding the trumpet to a passive generation. Violent faith should be the "normal" Christian lifestyle.

—PASTOR SHIRLEY ARNOLD
SHIRLEY ARNOLD MINISTRIES
FOUNDER AND SENIOR PASTOR, TREE OF LIFE FAMILY CHURCH

Judy has captured in these pages the practical side of faith that will inspire all of us to believe in our dreams and aspire to use our untapped measure of faith. This is a must-read for the saint and the seeker. I love it.

—DR. MYLES E. MUNROE
NASSAU, BAHAMAS

TAKE IT BY FORCE!

JUDY JACOBS

Charisma
HOUSE
A STRANG COMPANY

TAKE IT BY FORCE! by Judy Jacobs
Published by Charisma House
A Strang Company
600 Rinehart Road
Lake Mary, Florida 32746
www.charismahouse.com

Cover design by Judith McKittrick

Cover photos © 2005 Aslan Studios, Inc.
All rights reserved.

Library of Congress Cataloging-in-Publication Data:
Jacobs, Judy, 1957-
    Take it by force / Judy Jacobs.
        p. cm.
    ISBN 0-88419-958-4 (pbk.)
1. Christian life--Biblical teaching. I. Title.
  BV4501.3.J33 2005
  248.4--dc22   2005010042
  ISBN-13: 978-0-88419-958-8

07 08 09 10 —10 9 8 7
Printed in the United States of America

DEDICATION

I DEDICATE THIS BOOK to my late godly parents, Johnson and Gaynell Jacobs, who raised twelve children in the face of many hardships and challenges, yet their faith and determination remained intact to show me the way to obtain a constant faith and fire for God.

I dedicate this book to my strong siblings and their families, who have been there to encourage "their baby," to intercede in prayer, and to set the ultimate example of what strong faith looks like.

I dedicate this book to my eldest sister, Doris, who encouraged me by saying, "Don't forget to journal. I believe that you are a writer." Your constant reminder has kept my dream alive, and now it is so incredible to see faith come into sight!

I dedicate this book to Jamie Tuttle, my wonderful husband, my partner in ministry, my editor-in-chief, my confidant, my constant encourager, and a wonderful father to our girls. He is a man of faith and consistency who has led the way as we have braved many storms together in the past twelve years. I will love you as the eternities pass. You are my impenetrable rock! (1436)

I dedicate this book to my beautiful girls, Judith Kaylee and Erica Janell Tuttle. You are only eight and five at this writing, but I am already in warfare for you. I know there is already a strong faith and powerful anointing on your lives. As long as there is breath, your dad and I will be fighting violently to see you come into the greatness that is in you. You are my heart!

Finally and foremost, I dedicate this book to the Lord and Savior of my life, Jesus Christ. Your faithfulness has been so great and constant in my life. My faith sees through a glass that is dark, but one day I will see everything just as clearly as You see into my heart right now. Forever Yours!

ACKNOWLEDGMENTS

I WOULD LIKE TO say a heartfelt thanks to my wonderful friend and sister in the Lord, Prophetess Juanita Bynum, for her friendship, her relentless pursuit to stay in the presence of the Father, and her passion to reach the nations with the uncompromised Word of the living God.

To Stephen Strang and the wonderful Strang Communications Company family. Thank you for this extraordinary opportunity to impact generations to come with the Word of God through this work.

Thanks to Lillian McAnally, my very proficient editor who was so very patient and encouraging all through this work. Most of all, Lillian, thank you for your prayers and sensitivity to what the Spirit of God wanted to convey to the body of Christ.

Thanks to Lawana Dearnell, my personal assistant throughout this book, who helped me meet my deadlines.

To all of the His Song Ministries staff that has encouraged me, pitched in to help out, did research, and brought me in-house lunches, dinners, and late-night snacks. God bless you all!

To Eleanor Moodley, who has been so faithful to love and care for our girls and to be their friend when Mom and Dad couldn't be there. You are such a special gift.

To my family and the body of Christ who has given me permission to share your compelling stories of triumphant and struggle. The results will be worth it to see the lives changed because of this strong word and your powerful testimonies.

CONTENTS

FOREWORD

W HEN I WAS asked to write the foreword for this book, I struggled with the writing because I had so much in my spirit to
say—both about the author and her topic. I honestly did not know
where to begin. Like you, I have watched Judy Jacobs minister on
many major platforms and at countless conferences on the Trinity
Broadcasting Network. Whenever I have watched Judy, one thing is
always apparent: this lady has had an experience with God and knows
whom she is singing about! *Judy's anointing has been tested and proven
in the deep waters of violent faith.*

It also takes extreme faith to write a book. Let me tell you why.
Books that are written to bring spiritual restoration, such as Judy's,
must be written by the spiritually mature. Galatians 6:1–2 says:

> Brethren, if any person is overtaken in misconduct or sin of any sort,
> you who are spiritual [who are responsive to and controlled by the
> Spirit] should set him right and restore and reinstate him, without
> any sense of superiority and with all gentleness, keeping an atten-
> tive eye on yourself, lest you should be tempted also. Bear (endure,
> carry) one another's burdens and troublesome moral faults, and in
> this way fulfill and observe perfectly the law of Christ (the Messiah)
> and complete what is lacking [in your obedience to it].
>
> —AMP

This scripture gives two basic foundational principles for authentic Christian authors like Judy. First, she is covered by a mandate and
confirmed by a burden to bring restoration to God's people. Second,
the words that have been birthed out of her in writing have truly
come by the inspiration of God *because she is responsive and controlled
daily by the Spirit.*

How do I know this book is an authentic guide that will help you to take back by force what rightfully belongs to you? While I was in Florida finishing the manuscript for my newest book, *My Spiritual Inheritance,* I went out with my family one evening to a mall. I raised my voice while talking and felt something pop in my throat. My voice would no longer rise above a whisper. It was gone. To make things worse, the pain was so severe I could barely stand up.

They rushed me to the emergency room, where I was told that I merely had a bad infection. But three weeks later, after taking all of the medication, I still could not speak above a whisper. To make a long story short, I was recommended to a specialist in Nashville, Tennessee. After giving me a thorough examination, she explained that a cyst had erupted in one of my vocal cords and that I would most likely never regain my vocal range. If, by some divine chance, my voice came back, it would require at least one year of intense vocal training to be able to speak without experiencing pain. She continued by saying that therapists could possibly restore my speaking voice gradually, but that I would have to accept my range would always be different because one of my vocal cords had suffered a bad tear, which left it paralyzed.

I sat in that office watching an image of my vocal cords on the screen, one side moving properly and the other side remaining motionless. It was unbelievable. Fear gripped my heart. I thought, *Singing and preaching have been the center of my life and service to the Lord. How could it be possible that I would not be able to minister again with the gifts the Lord had given me?*

When I got back home I said, "OK, God, now what?"

The Lord's answer was simply, "Be found faithful in what I have called you to do."

At the time I was conducting a weekly Tuesday morning prayer meeting at five o' clock. Remembering the word of the Lord, I would go every Tuesday, unable to speak, and just lie on the floor weeping before Him. For six months I could not preach or sing, and I still could not speak above a whisper without pain. Then one Monday morning my cell phone rang. I rushed across the room to answer it, but by the time I had the phone in hand, I had missed the call. I thought, *Oh, well; I will just check the message later.* The Spirit of the Lord stopped me in my tracks and prompted me to check the message right then.

When the message started playing I heard Judy's voice. She said, "Juanita, I just came out of prayer, and I have a word from the Lord." She began to shout radically to the Lord and to declare, "This condition in your throat ends today!" She declared that God was giving me a new vocal cord and yelled violently at Satan, commanding him to take his hands off of my throat. While listening to Judy's message I collapsed under the power of God, weeping. When I was finally able to get back up on my feet, I grabbed the phone and pushed "save" to keep her powerful and encouraging message. Little did I know that simple touch of a button would mark history.

The next day (Tuesday) I went to early morning prayer doing what I had done for six months. I walked in, lay on the floor, and began to worship God in my spirit because I still could not speak. Moments later I heard the Spirit of the Lord say, "Get up, get the microphone, and preach. I sent the women of God into intercession for you, and I healed you yesterday." Once again, I began to weep. I stood up in obedience, took the microphone in my hand, and began to speak. A long, wailing sound came out of my mouth as if my voice was traveling back to me from some faraway place. I felt as if it was being freed from a deep, remote cave.

After that awesome day, I began preaching and singing again. Look at what God has done! My singing range is even higher *now* than it was *before* I lost my voice.

This book is vitally necessary reading for every believer, because those who are on the front line for the kingdom of God are not just being attacked—we are being *violently* attacked. I for one am blessed that Judy clearly understands the biblical principle of not just how to do battle in prayer, but to discern the level of a spiritual attack and return the right degree of force to counteract that attack. She knows how to prevail, disarming the enemy and setting the captives free!

Why do you need to read this book? There will come a time in your life when you, or someone you know, will be given the task to stand firm in the face of opposition and take back by force all that the enemy has stolen from you. Armed with the principles Judy shares in this book, you *can* refuse to give up, and you can stand firmly believing the promises of God. This book will empower you to clearly understand Matthew 11:12:

> And from the days of John the Baptist until the present time, the kingdom of heaven has endured violent assault, and violent men seize it by force [as a precious prize—a share in the heavenly kingdom is sought with most ardent zeal and intense exertion].
>
> —AMP

We, the people of God, will suffer violence, but in order to win decisive spiritual battles for His kingdom we must rise up, stand firm in our faith, and *take back by force* God's victory for ourselves and our families.

As you read this book and apply the biblical principles that Judy shares, you will discover that you can activate God's written and revealed Word and literally shift the course of events to line up with the perfect will of God! *Mark this day on your calendar,* for if you receive the ministry that God has birthed out of His anointed vessel with an open heart, your life will never be the same.

—JUANITA BYNUM

INTRODUCTION

THERE IS NOTHING more effective on the face of this earth than the power of prayer and the far-reaching hand of faith. Prayer and faith fit together like a beautiful symphony of orchestral music. Never underestimate them, for they have altered the course of nature, changed the laws of the universe, and have even influenced and changed the mind of God.

Having grown up in a home that was inundated with prayer, I understand its power. Mentored in a life of prayer by godly parents, family, and the covering of a home church, I have been able to see the impossible come to pass through the simple eyes of faith, and I will forever be affected.

I also understand what it means to tarry in prayer and wait before God in anticipation of seeing prayers answered. I remember as a small child falling asleep in the pews, and as I approached my adolescent years, I really didn't look forward to being in those "all-night prayer meetings." However, as I began to mature in stature and in the Lord, I saw the necessity of persevering and tarrying in prayer. One thing that I realized early on in life was that prayer and faith *really* work!

Another part of that prayer culture that I have seen and with which I have been involved was seeing the manifest miracles come forth as a result of prayer and faith. Having witnessed those healing meetings in the early sixties, I saw people bring their loved ones from far distances to get them in those meetings where the atmosphere was charged with the power of God. People were healed instantly.

I can remember as a small child, during the old camp meeting days, the sawdust floors, the organ music swell, the large choir with their hymnbooks, and the expectancy of the crowd that was hovering in the air wondering, *What's going to happen tonight? What miracle will we see?* I was fascinated to see people coming in wheelchairs and moments later leaping out of them. I loved watching emergency medical technicians drive those hearse-like ambulances onto the grounds, trying to help bedridden people get into the service with their cots. Hours later I witnessed them getting up and running around in their bedclothes, totally healed by the power of God.

People came from everywhere to experience these mighty moves of God. It was a time in our culture when people lived simple lives with childlike faith. Medical science had not advanced to the levels that it is today. People were not accustomed to going to the doctor unless it was a matter of life and death. If they had an incurable disease they trusted God to heal them, and, quite frankly, if God chose not to heal them, then there was no hope.

I have seen my parents do things that were uncommon in the sight of some people, because they were determined to see the purpose of God established. They were believing for miracles and breakthroughs in their lives and in the lives of their families and community. As I look back, I don't ever remember them polling public opinion to get permission to do what God told them to do. They knew that in order to see the impossible they would literally have to do the unthinkable.

I recall seeing my mom, who battled with high blood pressure problems, go for weeks, fasting and praying, believing God to sustain her, as she pressed into God for certain needs in our lives, in our church, and in our community.

My dad, a sharecropper in North Carolina, suffered as a diabetic and would sometimes collapse from the heat during the summer time. Exhausted and struggling with headaches and many other side effects from fasting, he would wrestle in prayer as he labored on the farm, because he had consecrated himself to a fast. He would never stop to think about the repercussions of his diabetic state or what his doctor, neighbors, or even his family thought. He was determined to see God finish His work in the situation, whatever it was. He was set on doing his part to see the kingdom of God advance.

This book comes as a result of their passionate faith and influence on my life. They instilled a faith in me to believe and dare for the unbelievable. They encouraged me to go after the things of God with a resolute passion and zeal and to never look back. They taught the necessity of prayer and not only ordinary prayer, but also persistent prayer—the kind of prayer that didn't stop until results came, and believe me, results are exactly what I saw.

Coming from that kind of background to this post-9/11 age that we are living in now, I see how very vital it is to leave a legacy of prayer and faith to my children the way that I was taught—and not only to my children, but also to this generation that is coming behind me.

This kind of legacy believes God despite the circumstances and has the faith to stand on the Word of God when there is nothing left to stand upon. I want to leave a legacy of truth, integrity, godly character, honesty, godly compassion, and a fiery zeal to seek God with a passionate fervor, so that this generation will see even greater miracles than I could have ever dreamed possible. My prayer is that they would cry out to God for His glory and presence in their lives, and as a result, they will touch the generations of "those yet unborn" for the glory of God. (See Psalm 22:30–31, NLT.)

We are being exposed to a lot of talk about God, prayer, and faith now that we are living in this pressurized, fear-craven, terrorist-stricken society. We turn on our television and don't know what to expect from week to week. What terror-alert color code will our nation be under today? What will happen in the Middle East? Where will the terrorists strike next? More than ever before, it is "politically correct" to have some belief system of God or some form of God. It is even more acceptable to pray, as long as you are praying what the world deems as a non-threatening prayer or that which stays within the parameters of what is acceptable, which is no mention of Jesus Christ, the blood, or the cross.

This world is drowning in a sea of fear, hopelessness, depravity, promiscuity, and godlessness. They are looking for someone to throw them a life preserver, anyone who just looks like they know how to stay afloat in this sea called life. The church has to be wide-awake to the hurting, the forgotten, the lost, the lonely, and the abandoned. The scheme of the enemy is "to steal, kill, and destroy" this generation that has a promise of ushering in the return of our Lord and Savior, Jesus Christ.

Along with this recognition of our enemy, we must be fully convinced about our faith and our God. We must trust in the infallible Word of the living God, and the only God worth knowing, loving, and serving is Jehovah God, the creator and sustainer of everything that exists.

A NEW LEVEL OF FAITH

Much has been said about prayer, and much has been said about faith, but little has been said about the kind of faith that has the power to literally change situations in the natural realm. That kind of faith I refer to as "violent faith." So for the sake of this book, know that I'm not referring to acts of violence. I am talking about spiritual warfare and reclaiming by force—in the spirit—what rightfully belongs to you. In Exodus 32, Moses used this kind of faith on Mt. Sinai, when God was ready to destroy all the children of Israel.

Moses was on Mt. Sinai for forty days and forty nights, being instructed by God concerning the Ten Commandments. While waiting for Moses to return, the people became restless and asked Aaron to make them a graven image to worship. When God saw that the people were corrupting themselves with idolatry, He became very angry and proceeded to tell Moses what they were doing.

> Then the Lord said, "I have seen what a stubborn, rebellious lot these people are. Now let me alone and my anger shall blaze out against them... all."
>
> —EXODUS 32:9–10, TLB

But Moses besought Jehovah his God, saying:

> Stop your anger. Think twice about bringing evil against your people! Think of Abraham, Isaac, and Israel, your servants to

whom you gave your word, telling them "I will give you many children, as many as the stars in the sky, and I'll give this land to your children as their land forever."
—EXODUS 32:12–13, THE MESSAGE

So the Lord *changed His mind* about the harm which He said He would do to His people.
—EXODUS 32:14, NAS, EMPHASIS ADDED

This speaks of the kind of influence and faith that Moses had with God—the courage and, literally, the audacity to command God to "stop Your anger," and then to remind the God who had made the heavens and the earth of what He had said. It was the same kind of faith and boldness that God gave to Moses when He told Moses how to answer Pharaoh: "I AM THAT I AM…Thus shalt thou say unto the children of Israel, I AM hath sent me unto you" (Exod. 3:14). I believe that kind of faith is called "violent faith."

The phrase *violent faith* is really two words that are thrown together in Christian circles, and yet, it remains foreign in its definition to many believers. People tend to understand the word *violent* as defined in Webster's dictionary: "marked by extreme force or sudden intense activity." The word *violence* is defined as, "exertion of physical force so as to injure or abuse." We understand these terms in the wake of seeing that very thing take place before our eyes with the situation that happened at the Twin Towers and the Pentagon a short time ago.

Just as the definitions of *violent* and *violence* are used in the natural realm, they can also be used in the spirit realm. In a spiritual connotation, these words mean: "to bring forth a spiritual force that will be used to cause injury, damage, and total destruction to the forces of darkness, by reason of violating our rights, properties, and privacy as a child of the almighty God."

Then there is the word *faith*. We certainly comprehend the definition of the word *faith*, which is the very bedrock of our Christianity. Scripture plainly states:

Now faith is the substance of things hoped for, the evidence of things not seen.

—HEBREWS 11:1

For without faith it is impossible to please God.

—HEBREWS 11:6, NIV

The just shall live by faith.

—GALATIANS 3:11

But you may ask, "How are the two words—*violent* and *faith*—connected, and what do they have to do with me?" Please permit me to answer that question with a question.

What do you do after life has dealt you a hard blow? Maybe your husband served you with divorce papers, the bank foreclosed on your mortgage, or you have just had to file chapter thirteen on your business. Perhaps you have just had to sign papers to have your child, friend, or family member enter a rehabilitation center, and all of your hopes and dreams for that person have suddenly been dashed upon the rocks. What about the doctor's report that has just been handed to you that says, "You will surely die," or the wayward son or daughter who has just been diagnosed positive with the AIDS virus?

Here you are groping through a tunnel of darkness—darkness so dense that it feels like you can literally take hold of it and grasp it. You feel depressed, disillusioned, embarrassed, frustrated, bitter, and angry. You try to make sense of it all but to no avail. All of the feelings that I mentioned are quite normal, and they are also to be expected when you face those kinds of storms.

Here is what God wants you to know. He wants to get involved with you right where you are in the midst of your storm. Through the power of prayer and exercising violent faith, you can be assured that things are about to change *if* you will have the courage to change your fear into faith—violent faith.

I believe that God wants to catapult you to a place of faith that is beyond wishful thinking and beyond the boundaries of religion and tradition. It even goes beyond the definition of what *you* understand faith to be. He invites you to go into the lions' den with Daniel and see God close the mouths of the lions. See yourself in the fiery furnace with Shadrach, Meshach, and Abednego, with not even the smell of smoke on their clothes. Go into the king's chamber with Esther, all the way whispering under her breath, "If I die, I die." Then watch as the king extends the golden scepter to her.

God wants to bring you to a level of faith where you are not moved by anything. He wants to bring you to a place where *your* prayers and violent faith usher in a boldness and an authority that will defeat the powers of darkness in your life and will ultimately determine the outcome of your situation.

GOD OF THE MIRACLE

Oswald Chambers in his book *My Utmost for His Highest* wrote, "Deliverance from sin is not the same as deliverance from human nature. There are things in human nature, such as prejudices, that the saint can only destroy through sheer neglect. But there are other things that have to be destroyed through *violence*, that is, through God's divine strength imparted by His spirit."[1]

I think the revelation that God wants to infuse into your spirit and mind through this work is that His strength is available to destroy those things in your life, no matter what they may be. He wants to see victory come in your situation through the power of *His* Holy Spirit and your faith.

Many times people seek out individuals, pastors, and even personalities, searching for answers to life's most difficult questions. Expecting "quick fixes," they want someone to wave their hand over them or touch them, much like Naaman, the Syrian leader, did with the prophet Elisha. Naaman was commander in chief of the Syrian army and was also very much admired and respected, but he had leprosy. He had heard that there was a prophet in Israel who could heal him, so he went to his house loaded down with gifts. But when he got there, he found things were not going as he had expected them to go.

> So Naaman arrived with his horses and chariots and stood at the door of Elisha's home. Elisha sent a messenger out to tell him to go wash in the Jordan River seven times and he would be healed of every trace of his leprosy! But Naaman was angry and stalked away. "Look," he said, "I thought at least he would come out and talk to me! I expected him to wave his hand over the leprosy and call upon the name of the Lord his God and heal me!
>
> —2 Kings 5:9–11, TLB

Naaman wanted the *miracle* but not the *God* of the miracle. He needed a lesson in humility and obedience, and Elisha was the man that God used to teach him that lesson. The Bible says that, "God is not a man" (Num. 23:19), and He certainly wasn't going to let man get the credit for His work.

> For my thoughts are not your thoughts, neither are your ways my ways, saith the Lord. For as the heavens are higher than the earth, so are my ways higher than your ways, and my thoughts than your thoughts.
>
> —Isaiah 55:8–9

Even though there is nothing wrong with seeking out people of faith to agree with you on a certain matter, there is something wrong when you can't go to God for yourself, by yourself, if you have to, and exercise *your* faith in the matter and see results.

There will come a time, if you haven't already been there, when there won't be anybody left but you and God, and usually that is how God sets it up. But you and God are the majority: "What shall we then say to these things? If God be for us, who can be against us?" (Rom. 8:31).

I can tell you that from my own experiences it has been "precept upon precept, line upon line…here a little, and there a little" and "from faith to faith" (Isa. 28:10; Rom. 1:17). It is believing God through His written Word and having the courage and boldness to look demons and devils in the face and plead the blood of Jesus Christ over my situation. With violent faith and persevering prayer, we can literally go to the gates of hell, knowing we're not going there by ourselves, and "snatch from the fire" those things that belong to us and our families (Jude 23, TLB).

Someone once said, "When you're going through hell, don't stop!" When you are going through a difficult time in your life, keep walking, keep going, because on the other side of your faith and obedience are the miracle and the breakthrough that you've been praying and believing God for. Be determined in your faith that you will not stop believing or give into doubt, but rather you will "fight the good fight of faith" (1 Tim. 6:12). Keep right on walking, because you are going to come through triumphantly, victoriously, and a winner.

My prayer is that as you take hold of this revelation, God will infuse your mind to think the way that He thinks and to see His purpose brought forth in your situation. What I have learned is that everything that God demands of you, He supplies to you. He told us, "[I] will supply all your need" (Phil. 4:19).

Be encouraged in knowing that "God hath dealt to every man the measure of faith" (Rom. 12:3). That "faith level" may feel small and insignificant now, but little becomes much with God. God stands ready to arm you with His mighty weapons.

> The weapons of our warfare are not carnal, but mighty through God, to the pulling down of strong holds.
> —2 Corinthians 10:4

The devil is a defeated foe in your life, and it's time you let him know that. Get ready for God to grab hold of you and shake you to bring forth a mighty miracle through you and in you. And, by all means, keep on walking!

You know what [a critical] hour this is, how it is high time now for you to wake up out of your sleep (rouse to reality).

—ROMANS 13:11, AMP

Chapter One

A RUDE AWAKENING

E ARLY ONE SUNDAY morning on the hillside of a tropical paradise known as Oahu in the Hawaiian Islands, children were chasing their kites and enjoying the bright sunshine. Some people were sitting in dentist chairs, housewives were sipping their second cup of coffee, and U.S. soldiers in Pearl Harbor were preparing for their daily regimen. For the locals, it was life as usual although the rest of the world was at war—a war that we were about to be pulled into. The United States was restless and uneasy about Hitler and his Nazi soldiers invading Europe, killing millions of Jews and democratic ideals.

Suddenly, the island began to rumble and shake; it felt as if the ground beneath their feet was about to cave in. People started running frantically, looking for shelter. Was it an earthquake or a volcanic eruption? It was neither. Unexpectedly, a swarm of carrier-based Japanese planes eclipsed this calm, peaceful Sunday morning like locusts. At the same time, Japanese submarines were attacking the United States Pacific fleet in the Hawaiian Islands, which disturbed the beautiful, blue, calm waters of the harbor.

The Japanese planes also attacked nearby military airfields. Eight American battleships and thirteen other naval vessels were sunk or badly damaged, almost two hundred American aircraft were destroyed, and approximately three thousand naval and military personnel were killed or wounded. Through national tragedy, a "sleeping giant awoke."[1] Our country had faced a very rude awakening. It was a critical hour. December 7, 1941, was indeed "a day of infamy" in our history. We have never forgotten the sacrifices made, and we will never forget.

I wasn't born yet when the Japanese attacked our forces in Pearl Harbor, but I was a witness to another rude awakening that our nation would face. The "sleeping giant" was about to have another wake-up call.

The morning was crisp and beautiful; you could almost feel the autumn season trying to shimmer its way through the sleepy, September morning. As I was going about my usual morning routine, a telephone call came in. I turned on the television, and if I close my eyes right now, I can still see the horrible, graphic images that were coming into my house through my TV set. Glued to my chair, I sat there in disbelief of what I was witnessing. I froze, but yet part of me wanted to run out of the house and go help these people. As I saw the first tower collapse, every hair on the back of my neck stood up; I felt helpless and totally vulnerable.

We have seen the images time and time again, and relived the pain, the shock, the horror, the disbelief, and the disillusionment. We cried out, "No! Not us! Not here in America!" The World Trade Center, the Pentagon, and possibly the White House were under an attack. All of these facts were overwhelming and somehow surreal. It was a critical hour for our nation again.

This country was rudely awakened to a terrorist attack. Terrorists? Here in the United States? Who were they? Where did they come from? Osama bin Laden? Who is that?

It is hard for me to comprehend the dark cloud that is hanging over our country as a result of one man and his nineteen chosen disciples who attacked us on September 11, 2001. The fact of the matter is that our president and his cabinet have been "roused to reality" and rudely awakened to the fact that America is subject to terror attacks simply because someone disagrees with our belief system. Now we must stand alert at our borders, in our cities, and, yes, even from day to day, ready to defend these United States of America. We are vulnerable people, living in "perilous times."

JESUS IS RUDELY AWAKENED

It had been a long, hard day for Jesus as recorded in the Gospel of Mark. Mark 4:35 begins with what scholars refer to as "the busy day," because it includes everything from Mark 3:22 through Mark 5.

To start His day off, the scribes and the Pharisees confront Jesus, accusing Him of being full of the devil and casting out devils by the prince of the devils (Mark 3:22). How is that for starters? Imagine that: Jesus starts His day off by being accused of demonic possession.

Next, His mother and brothers come looking for Him, and Jesus asks the question, "Who is my mother, or my brethren? . . . Whosoever shall do the will of God" (Mark 3:33, 35).

Then He began to teach by the seaside all the different parables (Mark 4:1–34). All of this took place throughout the stretch of what is known as the "same day."

At the end of the day, He says to His disciples, "Let us pass over to the other side" (Mark 4:35), and boards a ship. Assuming that His day probably started at around 3:00 a.m. communing with the Father, I'm sure by this time all He wants to do is nap. The Bible says that things were about to get a little bumpy.

> And there arose a great storm of wind, and the waves beat into the ship, so that it was now full.
>
> —MARK 4:37

Jesus is at the stern of the ship fast asleep. His faithless followers were in a very ominous situation, so they do the only thing they knew to do. They go and very rudely awaken Jesus from His peaceful rest. I can't imagine Peter and the other disciples going to Jesus and whispering, "Uh, excuse me, Jesus. We don't mean to wake you up, but we seem to have a problem here." No. I believe they were fumbling over each other to Him, shaking Him, and, terrified with fright, frantically shouting, "Teacher, don't you even care that we are going to drown?" (Mark 4:38, NLT).

Aroused from His rest, He gets up, speaks to the wind and the waves, and says, "Quiet down!" And the Bible says, "there was a great calm" (Mark 4:39, NLT).

Now, here is what you need to know.

Jesus knows how it feels to be rudely awakened to storms. He was there at Pearl Harbor; He was in the gas chambers in Nazi Germany during the Holocaust, when millions of His own people were literally destroyed. And yes, He was in New York City on 9/11 when the Twin Towers came crashing down. He was at the Pentagon and in that lonely field in Pennsylvania. He is also there with you—*right now*—in the midst of your storm.

When He rebuked the storm that day on the ship, He wasn't rebuking God the Father or Himself; He was rebuking the storm. It was a storm that was sent and caused by Satan himself to aggravate, disrupt, or maybe even to kill Jesus, and if not Jesus, then one of His disciples. Because Satan is the prince of the power of the air and can cause storms by the permission of God, as we see in Job 1:12–19 and Ephesians 2:2, that tells me that storms are inevitable in this life, and they will come.[2] Jesus said:

> In the world you have tribulation and trials and distress and frustration; but be of good cheer [take courage; be confident, certain, undaunted]! For I have overcome the world [I have deprived it of power to harm you and have conquered it for you].
>
> —JOHN 16:33, AMP

The question is not whether a storm will come and who will be the author of it, but rather the question is, how will you handle it when it does come? What will you draw from to get your strength and encouragement?

YOUR RUDE AWAKENING

You may have been gingerly going through your normal workday routine. But then came the telephone call, the interruption, the unexpected visitor, or the e-mail, something sent from Satan himself to you to rudely awaken you out of the slumber of your "ordinary" day. Now it is a critical hour for you.

Allow me to encourage you by saying we are not the only ones to ever be rudely awakened out of our euphoria. The Bible gives many examples of people who thought they were just floating on through life when they experienced a rude awakening.

- In Judges 16:20, Samson knew that feeling of snugness. When it came time to fight the Philistines, however, the Bible says "he shook himself" and found that the presence of God had departed.

- In 1 Samuel 15:23, it was Saul who lost his kingdom in one day because of his disobedience to do what he was told to do by the prophet. At that moment, God had already picked his predecessor.

- In 2 Samuel 12, David was roused to reality when the prophet Nathan, with a word from the Lord, visited him. David learned that to take his eyes off of God and to look with lust on something that didn't belong to him meant that there was a very high price to pay.

But later you hear a very humbled man cry, "Restore unto me the joy of thy salvation" (Ps. 51:12).

Our lives are so full of unexpected scenarios that we can suddenly become overwhelmed with situations that creep up on us and jar us to reality in just a brief moment. One minute our lives are like a very calm river flowing peacefully and smoothly, and, just like that, those calm waters become raging white rapids, the water is cold, and the future looks uncertain. Let me share with you our storm story.

Our Rude Awakening

I was ministering at Trinity Broadcasting Network during their fall telethon in November 2002. It had been a great night, and we were getting ready to go off the air when I noticed I didn't see my husband, Jamie, anywhere. Usually he would be right within eyeshot of me, but for some reason, I couldn't find him. As soon as the program ended, I was making my way to the green room when, suddenly, out of nowhere, Jamie came up from behind, took me by the arm, led me to a private area, and told me to sit. I knew by his expression and diligence that something was wrong.

As a mother, the first thing that came into my mind was, of course, my two girls at home with their caregiver.

"Are the girls OK?"

"Yes," he said.

Then I asked, "What's wrong?"

He replied, "I just got off the phone with your family. It's your sister Mary Lonie. They think that she has had a brain aneurysm."

Immediately my thoughts raced as I remembered hearing that same week about a similar situation in which a young mother who had suffered an aneurysm did not survive. I knew that it was a serious situation, and these kinds of attacks usually meant a death sentence.

Jamie began to assure me that the family was with her, and they were all praying and believing God for a miracle. With my face in the floor and crying out to God, I was desperate for answers.

"It just can't be, not her. Please, God, intervene."

This is the sister who is closest to me in age. We are a little over a year apart. We had grown up together in our family of twelve, and we were the "survivors," being the last two of the bunch. Growing up, she has been my coach, my pal, my defender, and my fighting buddy. But most of all, she is my sister whom I love and have looked up to all of my life. Mary Lonie is the strong one, the fearless one, the talented one, the smart one, and the leader. Me, well, I was the follower and the baby.

She and her husband have a great marriage, a beautiful daughter, and a lovely home. She is very much loved by everybody, from her church family to her neighbors and her kindergarten music class.

Just one month earlier our family had been rudely awakened and had come under major spiritual attacks. I had one sister who was just getting past the trauma of breast cancer, while another one had just been diagnosed with it. Although the first sister came out with a miracle, in which God supernaturally intervened and left the doctors astounded, my other sister, however, had received the news that she would need to have a mastectomy. In a time when we were just getting over those bad reports, all hell broke loose.

Trouble. No one is immune from it. Everyone who lives in this fallen state called life is going to meet up with it. Job said, "Man that is born of a woman is of few days, and full of trouble" (Job 14:1). Peter gives us some assurance when he says, "Don't be bewildered or surprised when you go through the fiery trials ahead, for this is no strange, unusual thing that is going to happen to you" (1 Pet. 4:12, TLB).

I'm glad that Peter didn't stop there in his admonitions, because later in chapter 5, he goes on to tell us where these troubles are coming from.

> Be careful—watch out for attacks from Satan, your great enemy. He prowls around like a hungry, roaring lion, looking for some victim to tear apart. Stand firm when he attacks. *Trust the Lord....* After you have suffered a little while, our God... personally will come and pick you up, and set you firmly in place, and *make you stronger than ever.*
>
> —1 PETER 5:8–10, TLB, EMPHASIS ADDED

David said:

> Many are the afflictions of the righteous, but the LORD delivereth him from out of them all.
>
> —PSALM 34:19

My sister Mary Lonie had been given a specific word from the Holy Spirit for the sister who earlier that week was diagnosed, and Mary Lonie felt prompted to deliver it in person. So she went to her home, along with my family, and she began to minister to her. As soon as she had delivered this word of encouragement to her, the attack came. She was struck down to the floor with a headache that felt as if her head would explode. To me, the devil had unleashed on her a very heinous act of violence because she chose to walk in total obedience.

Standing there in the TBN Atlanta studio, I felt overwhelmed, emotionally torn as to what I should do. Should I leave the studio, fly to North Carolina, and be with her and the rest of the family for the week, or should I stay and continue in ministry? I felt so desperately that I needed to be near her, and yet, I felt it would be just what the enemy wanted me to do: to leave my post in ministering to the nations.

After hearing how the attack came about, something within me rose up, and the only way that I can define it is "violent faith." The first thought that I had was, *How dare he do this to her while she was ministering to our sister.* At that point, I knew that I wasn't supposed to go anywhere, but I was to stay and sing into those cameras and do damage to the forces of darkness that had so violently attacked my sister.

Although my heart was troubled, my spirit was fixed, and I was determined to fight the darkness by singing and ministering to the nations through those television cameras. I was unyielding in my stance. The devil was not going to have my sister, and I wasn't going anywhere, but I was adamant about doing warfare for her in the spirit realm.

For the rest of that week I stared into those cameras declaring, "There's no God like Jehovah, there's no God like Jehovah."

The devil kept telling me, "You're going to look like a fool when your sister dies. Here you are singing on television when you could have been with her in her final moments."

I kept telling the devil, "Well, even if she were to die (which she is not), you're not going to get her. And look what's happening: there are people being born again, set free, and delivered, and you are losing big time. And what you meant for destruction, God is turning it all around for our good." At that point, he shut his mouth. Let me tell you that there is a way to silence the devil.

So along with my great friend Karen Wheaton, we began to call forth the healing power of God to my sister's life. We began to take back her life and to declare that she would be just as before. We were determined that we would not accept anything other than total victory. God even showed Karen a vision of my sister on the surgery table. In this vision, at one end of the table was the Father, instructing the surgeon, telling him exactly what to do. At the other end was Jesus, praying to the Father on her behalf, and hovering above her was the Holy Spirit. Then she saw the whole suite filled with ministering angels as they were ministering to her during the surgery.

Yet I couldn't help but wonder what she was going through at that very moment. I'll let her tell you in her own words.

When I reached my hometown hospital, they performed a CAT scan, and the diagnosis was a brain aneurysm, and it had bled twice. (Usually a person dies the first time that it bleeds.) My husband and I were immediately told that this hospital could not accommodate me and that I would have to go to Duke University Medical Hospital where a neurosurgeon would have to operate.

I was immediately carried by ambulance, not knowing that I would even survive the two-hour drive. I was told that there was so much blood on my brain that they probably could not get it all, and, if they were to leave me as I was, I would not last more than twenty-four hours. They also told me if they did operate, I could be left paralyzed, since the aneurysm occurred on the left side of my brain, which controls all my motor skills. The worse part of the operation was that I may not make it through the operation at all, because of the condition of the blood vessels.

Feeling a sense of hopelessness and despair, my sister was thrust into this oblivion, feeling the fingers of death grabbing at her from every place she looked. Along with that feeling, Satan kept reassuring her that if she didn't die, then she would be stuck with the reality of being paralyzed and unable to play the piano and organ again. He spewed out lies to her that she would never be the same wife and mother as before, and she would never be able to function as before.

All the while, we had called intercessors from around the globe to begin to intercede—Pastor Rod Parsley's intercessors, Benny and Suzanne Hinn's intercessors, and the Trinity Broadcasting Network family of intercessors, along with our home churches.

Meanwhile, my family embarked into the intensive care unit chapel and began to call on heaven. They knew that these were critical moments. They would not rest, and they would not let God rest until they saw positive results. Isaiah 62:7 says, "Take no rest, all you who pray, and give God no rest" (TLB).

After my sister said her good-byes to her family, she was wheeled away into the surgery suite, waiting for the anesthesiologist to come and administer the medicine. She later told us that all of hell came into that room with every demon and devil that could be imagined.

These evil spirits began telling her one lie after the other: "You're going to die; you made it through the aneurysm, but you won't make it through the surgery. We got you now. Where is your God now?" Struggling with an overwhelming sense of hopelessness, she didn't know what to do, so she began to pray in tongues. As she was praying in tongues, all of a sudden the Spirit reminded her of a dream that she had experienced days prior to this experience.

In this dream I saw a picture of myself in the hallway of our home. In this picture, I was an old woman, with many, many wrinkles. My hair had some color in it, but in my dream, I was a very old lady, and I thought to myself, *Wow! Look how old I am.* The next day when I awoke out of my sleep, I was so perplexed about the dream that I didn't even share it with my husband.

As I lay there on that bed in that surgery suite, the Lord reminded me of this dream and spoke to me and said, "Remember the dream? You're going to live to be an old lady with lots of wrinkles. You will not die, but you will live, to declare My wonderful works." With that reassurance, I filled that surgery suite with the praises of God, and I watched as the demons began to scream in terror and leave immediately. The Bible says, "Submit yourselves, then, to God. Resist the devil, and he will flee from you [in terror]" (James 4:7, NIV).

The next thing I knew, I was awake and saw my husband by my bedside. The first thing I wanted to know was, "Is it over?" He replied, "Yes, honey, and you are going to be fine!" I remember closing my eyes with the biggest smile on my face that I could make. Thank You, Father. You are so faithful!

In the Bible the devil is referred to in many ways, but the one thing that he is known for more than anything is the power to lie and to deceive. When he tells you that you are going to die, you need to tell him, "I shall not die, but live, and declare the works of the LORD" (Ps. 118:17).

When he tells you your children will not be saved, you need to remind him of what the Word declares:

> Believe in the Lord Jesus, and you will be saved—you and your household.
>
> —ACTS 16:31, NIV

When he tells you that you're going to lose all that you have, you need to tell him, "I'm blessed; blessed in the city, blessed in the country. I'm the head and not the tail, above only and not beneath; I go over and not under." (See Deuteronomy 28.)

When you hear a bad report that you are sick and cannot be healed, you need to declare, "By His stripes, I am healed" (Isa. 53:5).

When it seems like God is a million miles away, it is then that

He will show up in your dream, in your car, or in your surgery suite. One thing you need to know is that you are not alone.

Sometimes bad things happen to God's people! Maybe God has allowed this storm in your life to draw you closer to Him, so that you may know Him in a way that you never dreamed possible. If that is the case, then rest assured of His promise: "I will never leave thee, nor forsake thee" (Heb. 13:5).

If you are in a storm right now, I would encourage you to hold on with everything that you have, because when you come out of this thing, you will be stronger and bolder in your faith in God and more confident in what the Word says about you.

Maybe you have drifted from your walk with the Lord and allowed "things" to come between you and Him, and because you strayed, your "prize possessions" may have slipped through your fingers. Here are three steps that you can take to get back on course and to charter you and your family to safe waters once again.

STEPS TO AGGRESSIVE FAITH

1. Developing a righteous indignation

The first place to begin when you realize that the enemy has violated you is to turn the anger that you may be feeling in the right direction. Your anger should be directed to Satan himself, not your spouse, your children, your boss, or anyone who is made of flesh and blood.

The Bible declares that "we wrestle not against flesh and blood, but against principalities, against powers, against the rulers of the darkness of this world, against spiritual wickedness in high places" (Eph. 6:12).

The apostle Paul said, "Be ye angry, and sin not" (Eph. 4:26). What this verse implies is that God very clearly gave you a right to get angry. Getting angry is not sin. Matter-of-factly, anger is an emotion that originated from God, and we often find in the Scriptures where He became angry. (See Numbers 11:1; Psalm 7:11.)

What we can't allow is our anger to control us to the point where it causes us to get into bitterness, hatred, and malice, which lead to sin. Instead, we are to use that anger to develop a righteous indignation to see righteousness lifted up, sin destroyed, and Satan's schemes canceled against our lives and families. Be determined that things are about to change. Come to the point where you "have had it" with what the devil is doing in your life, and start to initiate change.

2. Assessing the damage

Sometimes athletes, and especially football players, never realize that they have been hurt in a game until the coach calls them to the sidelines or the bench and asks them to come out of the game. It is then that they realize that they have been playing with a broken finger, a stubbed toe, or something else. When the adrenaline is flowing, sometimes it is hard to know that you have been hurt.

It is the same way with life. Maybe you have found yourself as a single parent or single adult, or a person who was just passive and content to let people live their lives the way that they wanted to, and, as a result, things have really gotten out of control. In the midst of life, with the rush of trying to take care of everything and everybody, and seeking desperately to climb the corporate ladder of success, you have found yourself and your family out of church and away from God. Consequently, your life is a mess.

In your desperation and hopelessness, you are struggling to make sense of the time that you have been away from God. The next process for you is to step back, assess the damage and the time lost, and how it occurred.

Ask the Holy Spirit to reveal to you a plan and a process to get your crooked path straight again. John said, "Howbeit when he, the Spirit of truth, is come, he will guide you into all truth...he will shew you things to come" (John 16:13).

Remember that you can't do anything about the past except forget it (Phil. 3:13), but you can do everything about the future. So in order to go toward the future, you must assess the past and not repeat the same mistakes. The prayerlessness, not staying in the Word every day, and disassociating yourself from other believers have to change. All of these things draw us away from God and His presence.

The Scripture admonishes, "Looking unto Jesus the author and finisher of our faith" (Heb. 12:2). Make up your mind to surrender your entire being to God. Paul said, "For God is at work within you, helping you want to obey him, and then helping you do what he wants" (Phil. 2:13, TLB).

3. Damage control

If you have ever been around children, what is the first thing you do after an injury? If he's bleeding, you try to *immediately* stop the blood flow and calm the child. You assess the damage and take control of the situation. It is the same in the spirit realm.

Ask yourself some hard questions. Where did the breakdown occur between my husband and me? Where did my faith get lost? When did my relationship with the Lord begin to grow cold and indifferent? When did we stop going to church together as a family?

Then the only thing to do is to stop playing the blame game, ask the Lord to help you get your priorities back in order, and say as Joshua did, "As for me and my house, we will serve the Lord" (Josh. 24:15).

It will mean cleaning out your house of things that are not of God, instituting regular Bible and prayer times together, getting back in church, and trusting the Lord again. Get under the blood covering of the Lord again. You can be assured that the one thing that it will require is *change*. Paul said, "I *press* toward the mark for the prize of the high calling of God in Christ Jesus" (Phil. 3:14, emphasis added). It will require some pressing and stretching of yourself, so be prepared to cast off the old life and start afresh with new beginnings.

You have the power to stop the damage from getting any worse—not in your own strength, but through the power of God Himself. For you see, "When I am weak, then am I strong" (2 Cor. 12:10). When I don't have the power to do it alone, but yet I have the courage to confess my weakness to the One who is able to help me change it, that is when the change will occur. It is then that you will hear the voice of the Lord say, "My grace is sufficient for thee: for my strength is made perfect in your weakness" (2 Cor. 12:9).

Now that I have your attention, let's look at how we, as a nation, became passive and desensitized to the Spirit.

You may as well know this too, Timothy, that in the last days it is going to be very difficult to be a Christian. For people will love only themselves and their money; they will be proud and boastful, sneering at God, disobedient to their parents, ungrateful to them, and *thoroughly bad*. They will be hardheaded and never give in to others; they will be constant liars and troublemakers and *will think nothing of immorality*. They will be *rough and cruel*, and sneer at those who try to be good. They will betray their friends; they will be hotheaded, puffed up with pride, and *prefer good times to worshiping God*. They will go to church, yes, but they won't really believe anything they hear. Don't be taken in by people like that.

—2 Timothy 3:1–5, tlb, emphasis added

Chapter Two

A Passive and Desensitized Nation

D O YOU REMEMBER *The Andy Griffith Show* with Andy, Opie, Barney Fife, Goober, and Gomer Pyle? It is still, undoubtedly, one of my favorites. The show would always begin with that distinct, happy whistling tune while Andy and Opie, very pleasantly and cheerfully, walked down a country road with their fishing poles on their shoulders, smiling and looking so content.

Another favorite of mine was *Lassie*, the beautiful collie that was always saving someone and helping people get out of trouble. The thoughts that come to my mind are the wholesomeness of that era—the innocence, the simplicity, and the joy of sitting and watching something entertaining with your family without fear of embarrassment or disgust.

I am old enough to remember *The Ed Sullivan Show*. (OK, now I'm really telling my age.) Mr. Sullivan would have many entertainers on his program that varied from musical guests to circus acts. I also recall the time when Elvis Presley came on the scene of pop culture. Elvis would come on his program and shake and move his hips around to a beat that was labeled "rock 'n' roll." At that time, most people considered these gestures obscene.

Elvis's appearance on the show triggered public outcry from the viewing audience. People were outraged that this "kind of behavior" would be shown on television, and the public demanded that such vulgarity and promiscuity not be allowed on television. After that response, the cameras were not allowed to film Elvis from the waist down.

That didn't last long, however, because there would be many

others who would follow and would sink to even lower depravity than that. The more depravity we allowed into our homes and the more we bought their wares, the less we saw of our innocence as a nation.

We went from *The Andy Griffith Show* to *The Jerry Springer Show*, from *Lassie* to MTV. Even today's cartoons captivate our kids and encourage them to live a life of rebellion. Somewhere in between we became a passive and desensitized nation. But how did we get to that point?

THE SELF-ABSORBED NATION

Our nation is obsessed with drugs to the extreme of legalizing marijuana for medical purposes, whatever that means. We are living in a time when our government recognizes secular humanism but considers things such as the Ten Commandments displayed in public buildings, prayer in our schools, and the words *under God* in our Pledge of Allegiance unconstitutional. We are at a point where we embrace same-sex marriages and even allow same-sex couples to adopt children to try and create a so-called "normal" family. How did we reach this point in our society?

We live in a post-Christian era where "violence is glamorized in music, television, film, literature and video games. Virtually everywhere a young person turns, he encounters a culture that embraces violence. This toxic culture serves to desensitize kids to the brutality of violent behavior. By the time the average child leaves elementary school he or she has witnessed 8,000 murders and 100,000 other acts of violence on the television screen."[1]

In 1961 the movie *West Side Story* won the Academy Award for Best Picture. I remember how violent that the movie appeared to be to its viewers at that time. In *West Side Story*, gang members dressed up in suits and ran around shooting each other. Compare that to the blockbuster movie *Pulp Fiction* where violence is glamorized on the big screen.

Lt. Col. Dave Grossman in his book *On Killing: The Psychological*

28

Cost of Learning to Kill in War and Society argues that popular culture is literally training young people to kill very much in the same way that the military trains soldiers to kill. Because most humans have an innate aversion to killing another human being, Grossman says that the military must desensitize soldiers to killing and help them overcome that built-in aversion. By exposing soldiers to constant images of violence and brutalization, young recruits soon accept destruction, violence, and death as a way of life.[2]

Grossman goes on to say:

> In the same way, today's youth are exposed to these same images, slowly desensitizing them to the horror. Eventually, the images become less shocking and more acceptable. Those exposed to the images become increasingly comfortable with them, so that the built-in aversion to them is broken down.[3]

How vividly do we remember the dreadful deaths that took place at Columbine because of the influence of powerful animated video games?

Witchcraft and the occult are also popular among our young people. The popularity of witchcraft-oriented programs for young people proves that there is an entire generation of children becoming desensitized to the horrible world of the occult. The best-selling book series and blockbuster movie series Harry Potter is proof that this movement is growing among young people. This phenomenon has introduced literally millions of kids to young witches, wizards, and evil, and these kids are led to believe that witchcraft is fun, exhilarating, and innocent.

As a nation we are consumed with alcohol, vulgarity, pornography, and abortion on demand. Now with just one click of a button, any kind of filth or sinful pleasure imaginable can be found. Homosexual agendas are being shoved down our throats, while every day we become more anti-God and anti-Christian.

I believe in order for us to know where we are going, we must understand where we have come from. We didn't get to this stage overnight. It happened little by little, very subtly. Bit by bit we have allowed our Christian morals and values to be taken away from us.

THE LOSS OF INNOCENCE

When God first placed this message on my heart, I was very much disturbed about the things that I was hearing week after week from places where I would minister. It seemed as if God's people were void of any power and authority, and were struggling very deeply with discouragement and depression. They seemed to have settled with what was happening in their lives. Satan was using sickness, divorce, drugs, alcohol, and many other things to rip families apart. The disturbing thing to me was that no one seemed to know how all of this happened, and even worse than that, how to pray and bring change. It seemed that people had given up on ever seeing things any different. There was no hope, no faith, and consequently, no breakthroughs or miracles. Upon reading the opening chapter passage from 2 Timothy 3, anyone would think that Paul was describing our modern-day society. He describes so prophetically and graphically the very hour in which we are living.

I remember so clearly after a service one night, a mother came up to me with tears running down her face but with a look of disgust and determination. She said to me, "Judy Jacobs, you have made me mad tonight."

I froze in my steps and thought to myself, *Somebody, help!*

I tried to look composed and unshaken, not knowing what this lady was about to say or do. I said to her, "I did? How did I make you mad?"

She said, "My son is an alcoholic and a drug user and dealer. He steals from me, he pushes me around, and I had given up on that boy ever being saved." Then she said, "I love that boy, and when he was born, I dedicated him to God to be used by God, so the devil is not going to get him. When you began to speak about Matthew 11:12

and having violent faith to reclaim your property back through the Word of God and by exercising violence through the Spirit, I said, 'That is it; that is my son, and the devil is not going to have him. He belongs to me, and he belongs to God.' You have made me mad, and in Jesus' name, I'm going to take back my son."

I was thrilled to receive a letter weeks later from that mom testifying of God's saving grace on her son's life. Praise God, she got her son back! God is always moved by faith, and He will always honor and react to it.

The Word also reminds us that people would possess "a form of godliness," but they would deny the power of God. So Paul warns Timothy, "Don't be taken in by people like that." Don't hang around them; don't associate with them. It matters whom you hang around, because oftentimes the people you think are your friends turn out to be your biggest discouragers. So be careful with whom you fellowship.

Paul gives further instruction to Timothy: "But you must keep on believing the things you have been taught" (2 Tim. 3:14, TLB). When we were growing up, the rules that we were given and the lines that were drawn in our family were not a choice. We obeyed because God gave us God-fearing parents who taught us the Word of God, spoke into our lives, and believed that if you "spared the rod, you spoiled the child." (See Proverbs 22:15.) We had to adhere to these principles, because these were the same principles that their parents taught them. And they worked!

Paul says, "We are not ignorant of his [Satan's] devices" (2 Cor. 2:11). The devil's joy would be to interrupt and wreak havoc on everything that is precious to us and destroy our lives as we know them.

One of the reasons why we find our lives in such a mess is that we become so absorbed with what society deems "politically correct" that we have become willing to throw our convictions—and at times, our common sense—out the window. Churches have practiced "tolerance" so much that sin is "tolerated" and accepted when what should be accepted is the *person—not the sin*. Sinners should feel accepted and welcomed in a church, but we shouldn't allow them to remain comfortable in their present state. We have forgotten the magnitude of the cost of Christ's blood.

We subject ourselves to movies that corrupt the family. We allow television programs into our homes that poke fun at anything that is considered holy and sacred to us, and we have replaced time spent with God in prayer, praise, worship, and the Word with meetings, ball games, and family entertainment.

Please don't misunderstand me; there is certainly nothing wrong with wholesome family entertainment, but there is something wrong when this entertainment takes us away from the time that is supposed to be dedicated to God.

A LOOK BACK

In the 1960s we as Americans were at peace with the world, essentially, and were very busy pursuing the American dream: a great job, a nice car, a house, two kids, and a dog. Americans became sold on the idea that their kids "would have more than I did growing up" and became consumed with the "almighty dollar." This period was known to be a time of decline in moral values and a rise in immorality and disrespect for authority.

A friend of mine, whose father was a well-known church leader during the 1960s, told me that he once asked his dad why most of our religious freedoms were taken away and why morality declined. He asked his father, "Dad, where was the church during those times?" His dad responded, "Son, we wrote letters to our senators and congressmen, and we trusted them that they would make the difference." But they didn't!

There was another radical movement during the 1960s, but this time it involved the church. It was called the Jesus People movement. We began to see a mighty revival begin to arise, and we were encouraged to see God beginning to move in our midst. The Pentecostal movement and the Charismatic movement began to surface, and the Holy Spirit began to be introduced in such an awesome way that denominational barriers began to fall. We began to see the church come together as never before.

But even with a mighty move of God, there are still some who become hard, critical, fault-finding, and, of course, apathetic. In 2 Timothy 3:1–5 (NAS), Paul lists eighteen characteristics to describe mankind's attitude in the End Times.

1. Lovers of themselves (self-centered, conceited, egotistical)
2. Lovers of money (greedy for money, avaricious)
3. Boasters (braggarts, full of great swelling words)
4. Proud (arrogant, haughty, overbearing)
5. Blasphemers (evil speakers, profane, abusive, foulmouthed, insulting)
6. Disobedient to parents (rebellious, undutiful, uncontrolled)
7. Unthankful (ungrateful, lacking in appreciation)
8. Unholy (impious, profane, irreverent, holding nothing sacred)
9. Unloving (hard-hearted, unnaturally callous, unfeeling)
10. Unforgiving (refusing to make peace, refusing efforts toward reconciliation)
11. Slanderers (spreading false and malicious reports)
12. Without self-control (men of uncontrolled passion, debauched)
13. Brutal (savage, unprincipled)
14. Despisers of good (haters of whatever or whoever is good; utterly opposed to goodness in any form)
15. Traitors (betrayers)
16. Headstrong (reckless, self-willed, rash)
17. Haughty (making empty pretensions, conceited)
18. Lovers of pleasure rather than lovers of God (those who love sensual pleasures but not God)

Maybe you're thinking, *OK; this is how our society arrived at such a lowly state, but what does that have to do with my situation?* I am so glad you asked.

THE APPREHENSION OF GOD

The reason that you have this book in your hands is because you are in pursuit of something. You are trying to apprehend the truth and answers to your questions, which can only be found in Christ.

Paul said in Philippians 3:12, "Not as though I had already attained, either were already perfect: but I follow after, if that I may *apprehend* that for which also I am *apprehended* of Christ Jesus" (emphasis added).

The apostle Paul remembered his "road to Damascus" experience, when he was literally knocked off of his horse. He knew at that point that he had been apprehended; he even knew who it was who had apprehended him. Paul's response was, "Lord, what wilt thou have me to do?" (Acts 9:6). God had apprehended Paul so that he would speak to the Jew *and* the Gentile.

The word *apprehend* means "to arrest or seize." For example, a police officer will apprehend you (or arrest you) if you commit a crime. When Paul wrote to the Christians at Philippi, he told them his goal was to take hold of the purpose for which God had "seized" him.

Now that God has apprehended you and you know the truth, you are responsible for what you know. God has gotten your attention, and the Holy Spirit has His hand on you. You need to rise up out of your complacency and take back what is yours. No more excuses! God has a plan for your life, your children, and your ministry. He says, "I know the thoughts that I think toward you...thoughts of peace, and not of evil, to give you an expected end" (Jer. 29:11).

The Word of God encourages us to press forward and move into a place of victory and maturity. Then we will come alive again and understand what is the Lord's will for our lives.

> Let us go on...to other things and become mature in our understanding, as strong Christians ought to be.
>
> —HEBREWS 6:1, TLB

Maybe He has apprehended you to fight for someone who is too little or too wounded to fight for themselves. Maybe He has apprehended you to shake yourself free from the apathetic lull that you find yourself in, or maybe He has apprehended you to seek after Him in a way that is beyond even your comprehension. Whatever the case may be, I know that something has been stirred within you to go after all that God has for you.

Regardless of all the "gloom-and-doom" news you hear, make no mistake about it: God is still in control. He is looking for a remnant that will go in the mighty name of Jesus and take back territories, cities, regions, and countries in His name and for His glory. He wants you. Are you ready? If so, change your stance, gird up your mind, and let's forcefully advance the kingdom of God.

What is faith? It is the confident assurance that something we want is going to happen. It is the certainty that what we hope for is waiting for us, even though we cannot see it up ahead.

—HEBREWS 11:1, TLB

But without faith it is impossible to please him: for he that cometh to God must believe that he is, and that he is a rewarder of them that diligently seek him.

—HEBREWS 11:6

So you see, it isn't enough just to have faith. You must also do good to prove you have it. Faith that doesn't show itself by *good works* is no faith at all—it is dead and useless.

—JAMES 2:17, TLB, EMPHASIS ADDED

Chapter Three

WHAT IS VIOLENT FAITH?

WE ALL KNOW that we are called to live by faith, but you may ask, "What is violent faith? Why do we need to use violent faith? What's wrong with just having faith? Isn't faith alone good enough?"

I believe that sometimes we come up against certain things in our lives when just maintaining won't be enough. Sometimes you have to do something out of the ordinary—go out on a limb, get out of your comfort zone, and, like Peter, get out of the boat and "walk on water." Sometimes you have to do *something!*

My definition of violent faith is "sheer determination, aggressiveness in the Spirit, an attitude of perseverance, and raw gutsiness." It is a spirit of going against the norm, going against the tide, public opinion, perception, and sometimes even common sense. Acting on faith does not always make common sense. Sometimes God will tell you to do something that doesn't make any sense in the natural.

So you see, it isn't enough just to have faith. You must also do good to prove that you have it. Faith that doesn't show itself by good works is no faith at all—it is dead and useless. But someone may well argue, "You say the way to God is by faith alone, plus nothing; well, I say that good works are important too, for without good works you can't prove whether you have faith or not; but anyone can see that I have faith by the way I act." Are there still some among you that still hold that "only believing" is enough? Believing in one God? Well, remember that the demons believe this too—so strongly that they tremble in terror! Fool! When will you ever learn that "believing" is useless without doing what God wants you to? Faith that does not result

37

in good deeds is not real faith....You see, a man is saved [and pronounced righteous before God] by what he does, as well as by what he believes....Just as the body is dead when there is no spirit in it, so faith is dead if it is not the kind that results in good deeds.
—JAMES 2:17–20, 24, 26, TLB

Faith alone without works is dead, which is why you need to exercise faith and put it into action. And when you do begin to walk in faith, expect the enemy to fight you.

THE WAR BETWEEN GOOD AND EVIL

Since the beginning of time as recorded in the Holy Scriptures, there has always been a fight between good and evil, between Father God and Satan (or Lucifer as he is referred to in Isaiah's recording of his downfall).

How art thou fallen from heaven, O Lucifer, son of the morning! how art thou cut down to the ground, which didst weaken the nations! For thou hast said in thine heart, I will ascend into heaven, I will exalt my throne above the stars of God: I will sit also upon the mount of the congregation, in the sides of the north: I will ascend above the heights of the clouds; I will be like the most High. Yet thou shalt be brought down to hell, to the sides of the pit.
—ISAIAH 14:12–15

In this passage, Isaiah is describing the heart of Satan in his quest to overthrow the throne of God. There are many ways Satan is described; he is referred to as "The Morning Star" or "Daystar," and "the bright one." Before his downfall, Satan was the worship leader, and when God wanted praise and worship, He would call upon Lucifer. Every imaginable instrument was found in his being, and besides that, he was obviously very popular in heaven to have had one-third of the angels to go with him in his rebellion. (See Revelation 12:4.)

The conflict between good and evil began in the heavenlies, came down to the Garden of Eden, and will end when Satan is thrown into the lake of fire to be there for eternity. The garden was a place of sheer perfection that God had designed for His creation to live in peace and harmony surrounded by everything and anything that they would ever need. It was a place where God Himself would come down "in the cool of the day" to have fellowship and communion with His creation (Gen. 3:8).

Satan strategically planned every move made there in the garden to assure the Fall of mankind, even in choosing to manifest himself as a serpent, which was more subtle than any beast of the field that the Lord God had made (Gen. 3:1). He persuaded them to eat of the forbidden fruit, promising that they would be like God, able to discern between good and evil (v. 5).

After partaking of the forbidden fruit, suddenly their eyes were opened to the sin that they had committed. This was a strategic point when the conflict between good and evil, God and Satan, began to accelerate.

Then God began to speak forth the punishments that would be incurred because of their disobedience. The first punishment is issued to the serpent, and rightly so:

> So the Lord God said to the serpent, "This is your punishment: You are singled out from among all the domestic and wild animals of the whole earth—to be cursed. You shall grovel in the dust as long as you live, crawling along on your belly. From now on, you and woman will be enemies, as will your offspring and hers. You will strike his heel, but he will crush your head."
> —GENESIS 3:14–15, TLB

To the woman, God said, "You will have great pain in childbearing," and to the man, "You will have to toil the land." There were lots of repercussions to all the disobedience in the garden, but the one indictment that stands out as the greatest was against Satan himself.

God said, "You will strike his heel, but he will crush your head" (Gen. 3:15, TLB).

> The woman's seed would crush the devil's head, a mortal wound spelling utter defeat. This wound was administered at Calvary when the Savior decisively triumphed over the devil. Satan, in turn, would bruise the Messiah's heel. The heel wound here speaks of suffering, and even of physical death, but not ultimate defeat. So Christ suffered on the cross, and even died, but he arose from the dead, victorious over sin, hell and Satan.[1]

Because of the beguilement with Eve that Satan so subtly and strategically planned, there has been this conflict between Satan and the woman ever since. The Bible very plainly stated, "From now on, you and woman will be enemies" (Gen. 3:14, TLB). Make no mistake about it, he hates women, and we hate him. The war is still waging. He is still after our stuff, our children, our marriages, our minds, and our bodies.

Satan is also our accuser, and he is constantly spitting out lies to us and to God.

- "You're not going to make it."
- "You shall surely die."
- "Your children are going to be lost."
- "You can't have a ministry."
- "You are not worthy."
- "Look how they are not praying enough."
- "Watch how they neglect Your Word; why, they don't even know it."

You have to remember that he is a liar and the father of lies. (See John 8:44.)

That is why we must fight back in our faith and strike back with force, because the only way to defeat him is by being aggressive in the spirit. Paul declared, "Fight the good fight of faith." If we are ever going to get our possessions back, we are guaranteed a fight. It is a story as old as Adam and Eve. He is still trying to get God, and once again, he is using God's children as human shields. His ultimate goal is to stop the plan of God in your life. He uses the oldest and most used tricks in the books, because they have worked for thousands of years.

But what the devil doesn't know is that you and I are going to use some things that are the oldest and most used tools in "The Book," that is, the Word of the living God, to send him reeling on his ears.

Because of the glorious victory on the cross, we are victorious in every area of our lives. God has made a way for us to live in this victory that He purchased for us. But He plainly states in Hebrews 10:38 the only way we can live in this victory: "Now the just shall live by faith."

WHAT IS FAITH?

One of the opening scriptures for this chapter was Hebrews 11:1:

> It is confident assurance that something we want is going to happen. It is the certainty that what we hope for is waiting for us, even though we cannot see it up ahead.
>
> —TLB

Faith is the absolute confidence that what I want and what I desire as a child of God is already mine, and it is going to happen. I don't have to think or wonder about it. I know what the Word says, and I stand on faith. When it seems there is nothing left to stand on, I still stand. I can't see it with my eyes, hear it with my ears, or touch it with my hands, but I know that God is faithful to His Word.

Faith is believing in spite of your circumstances and surroundings. No matter what your circumstance may look like, you have full confidence that what you are hoping for will come to pass. The enemy studies you closely so that he can pinpoint your weaknesses and use them against you. He can tell when you have a look of faith versus a look of doubt.

You may find yourself saying, "Well, I don't know. I guess I just got this from Mama. She had this disease, and I guess I was bound to get it sometime." That junk has to stop! You have to be fully persuaded that what God said about healing, or anything else concerning His children, He will do!

Generational curses were destroyed when Paul, under the inspiration of the Holy Spirit, declared, "Christ hath redeemed us from the curse of law, being made a curse for us: for it is written, Cursed is every one that hangeth on a tree: That the blessing of Abraham might come on the Gentiles through Jesus Christ; that we might receive the promise of the Spirit through faith" (Gal. 3:13–14).

Smith Wigglesworth, in a devotional book he wrote, says, "Faith is actively refusing the power of the devil"—refusing to give into his lies, refusing to accept his reports, refusing to give into the fear and depression, but actively standing on what God has said and what His Word has said.

EXPECT A MIRACLE

I will never forget a service where I was ministering this word on violent faith. The power of God moved in that place, and we all just began to worship. All at once I heard the Lord say to me, "I am healing people of cancer." As He spoke that word to me, I spoke it to the people. And just as it came out of my mouth, there was one lady in the back who immediately stood up on her feet and raised her hand. It wasn't her standing up that caught my attention, or the way that her hand went up like a lightning bolt, but it was the look of faith and determination on her face, which I had never seen before. She had obviously come expecting a miracle.

This lady had ovarian cancer and had already been through chemotherapy and radiation. As she stood there with a wig on her head to cover the hair loss from chemotherapy treatments, she had a fierce look of faith in her eyes.

The doctor had told her that she would be dead before Christmas that year. But I saw faith beaming out of her, and that look of faith was saying, "Yes, I have cancer. Yes, the doctor says I will be dead before Christmas, but things are about to change."

I said to her, "Ma'am, God is healing you right now," and with that, she fell to the floor. Thank God for the ushers who caught her!

Forty-five minutes later, she got up off the floor, ran around the building like a mad woman, and screamed at the top of her voice, "I'm healed! I'm healed! I'm healed!" And the whole time she was running, her daughter, who had brought her to the meeting, was running after her yelling, "Slow down, Mama, slow down." But there was no stopping this lady, because something very drastic had happened.

When Jesus touches you, there is no stopping you or slowing you down. Everyone around you knows it.

The very next week she went to her doctor and told him, "Please take another scan. God has given me a miracle."

The doctor was very hesitant and said to her, "Please don't do this to yourself. You know what the report says."

"Yes, I know what the report says," she said to him, "but I had this really wild Indian woman pray for me, and I know that God has healed me."

The doctor very reluctantly ordered another scan.

The very next Sunday she stood on the stage with her pastor, but this time with a look of joy, excitement, and victory on her face. In the one hand she held the scan that said she would be dead before Christmas, but in the other hand she held a scan that showed there was no cancer. Something miraculous had happened.

God wants to do the unthinkable, the undeniable, and the unbelievable through any person who will dare to believe Him with violent faith.

The Bible says that we walk by faith and not by sight. We can't fix our eyes on the natural, because in the natural, it doesn't look good. In Numbers 13, the twelve spies were sent out to spy the Promised Land for Moses. Ten of them saw in the natural, but there were two, Joshua and Caleb, who "had a different spirit," a violent spirit. Sure, they saw in the natural, but they looked beyond the natural and saw the supernatural. It didn't look good because there were giants there. But Joshua and Caleb didn't see it as an opposition. They saw it as an opportunity for God to be who He said He was to the children of Israel. They announced to Moses and the children of Israel, "Let us go up at once, and possess it; for we are well able to overcome it."

When you are faced with giants, don't deny them or pretend they're not there! No! You don't deny fact, but you believe truth. The fact of the matter is, in the natural, there are giants. You do have cancer, but the truth of the matter is, "By His stripes we are healed." And then declare as Joshua did, "I am well able to conquer it."

There will always be giants, and the bad news is the giants are getting bigger. The Bible says that evil men "shall wax worse and worse" (2 Tim. 3:13).

There will always be an opposition to your mission. If you don't believe me, then just try losing weight, and a doughnut shop *will* be built down the street from your house. If you are praying for your husband's salvation, he will rebel even more. If you pray for your children's salvation, they will go out and do something to embarrass you. There will always be an opposition to your mission that God has mandated. That is the reason why you can't walk in the natural, but in the supernatural. "The just shall live by faith" (Heb. 10:38). God has given us purpose, destiny, and promises, and He keeps and fulfills His promises. When you meet up with those giants, you have to have a spirit of David that says, "You come to me with a spear, a sword, and a shield, but I come to you in the name of the Lord." David met his Goliath, and the giant met his doom.

GET THE JUNK OUT!

God reminded me of something that happened to me on my journey to exercising violent faith and learning obedience.

I remember so vividly being very sick with bronchitis, which, according to my doctor, had turned into pneumonia. As I sat in the office of my Spirit-filled Korean doctor, he said to me in his broken

English, "Sister Jacobs, you very sick. You go to hospital. You need IV. You stay in hospital, oh, I don't know, maybe four or five days, maybe a week."

At this point in my walk with the Lord, I was unwavering in my determination to go to the next level in faith. I knew if I was going to see the sick healed and delivered, I personally would have to walk in healing and deliverance.

So I said to him, "No, doctor, you don't understand. God is going to heal my body. I can't go to the hospital. I must trust in God."

He said, "OK, but I not responsible."

I came home from that doctor's office even more adamant that something was about to happen with my faith level. Mind you, I wasn't having a whole lot of fun learning this lesson, but I wanted God and everything that He had for me, and I wasn't about to give up.

So here I was on my bed, isolated from my husband and my children. Completely miserable, I was surrounded by stuff everywhere on my bed. On one side, I had my Kenneth and Gloria Copeland faith tapes; on the other side, my Benny Hinn healing tapes; and in my lap, I had my Rod Parsley Breakthrough Covenant Partner Bible. I was doing everything I knew to do—praying in tongues, rebuking, casting out, planting seed, and calling forth—everything except turning somersaults. I would have done those too if I had felt like it. I was desperate, and when you get desperate enough, you will do anything.

I found myself so weak, I could hardly get out of bed to go to the bathroom by myself. My husband and I used walkie-talkies primarily as a communication tool for the two of us. I had one upstairs in my bed, and he had one downstairs. So if I needed anything, I would just mash this little red button on the walkie-talkie and call my husband, "Honey, I would love some orange juice, please," or "I'm ready for some lunch."

So here I was upstairs, believing for a miracle, expecting an angelic being to walk into that room at any moment and lay his hands on me. Then I would just get up, and that would be the end of it. But that is not what happened!

I was lying there so utterly miserable when I clearly heard the command of the Lord say, "Get up out of this bed, go downstairs, and command this junk to get out of your house and out of your body!"

I knew the voice of the Lord, and so I said to God, "OK, God, but I'm going to call my husband and tell him to do it. After all, he is the priest and the prophet in our house."

I had decided that I really didn't feel like getting up and going downstairs after being in the bed for three weeks. So, in my mind, I would get Jamie to come up and agree with me in prayer about what I had just heard the Spirit of God tell *me* to do. And just as I went to reach for the walkie-talkie, I heard the voice of the Lord in my spirit say even more forcefully, "Stop! I told *you* to do it!"

I got up from the bed that I had been in for three weeks, and, I must admit, I did not look pretty. I pulled my bathrobe on, slid into my house slippers, and went walking down the steps. I got halfway down the steps when it dawned on me what was really going on. I became very angry. All at once I realized that this was an attack from the devil to take me out.

When I got to the bottom of those stairs, I was fully convinced that I had a word from the Lord. My husband took one good look at me and recognized the fire in my eyes and the smoke that was seemingly coming out of my ears. He had been around long enough to know that, in the spirit realm, that meant trouble to the kingdom of darkness.

"Uh-oh," he said.

"You're exactly right," I said. "God spoke to me upstairs and told me to come down here and command this junk to get out of our house and out of my body, and that is exactly what I am going to do."

I walked over to our front door and opened it. It was in the middle of the dead of winter, but I didn't care. I stepped out onto the porch in my 101 Dalmatians pajamas and my hair sticking up in all different directions because I'd been in the bed for three weeks, but I didn't care. I had a word from the Lord, and I needed a miracle.

I lifted my voice as high as I could possibly lift it and said, "In the name of Jesus, bronchitis, pneumonia, and everything associated with it, get out of my body, and not only that, but every living germ that is present in this house, you have to go, too. You cannot stay, and you will not stay. On the authority of God's Word and through the name of Jesus, you will leave right now! This body is the temple of the Lord, and this house is dedicated and belongs to God. Right now I am going to fill this place up with praise and worship, and you have no choice except to leave."

All of a sudden I looked out across the street, and there were my neighbors walking their dog. They took one good look at me and started to walk their dog faster. I guess they thought I was screaming at my husband. I didn't care what they thought or what anyone else thought for that matter; I had a word from the Lord, and I needed a miracle. I knew that one word from God could change everything.

What I have learned, and I am still learning, is that I can't worry about what people say or think about me. I have to be obedient to the Lord and do what the Lord tells me to do, and so do you.

No matter how silly it may seem or how crazy it may seem, you must listen to the voice of God and do whatever He tells you to do. Just do it, because on the other side of your obedience and violent faith there is a breakthrough and a miracle waiting on you.

Immediately I felt an overwhelming breath flow through my body. It was as if someone had put an oxygen mask over my face, and I was breathing in fresh, living air. Then, just as suddenly, I noticed that my voice came back, along with renewed strength that came into my being. I cooked supper that night for my family. That kind of attack has not been back at my house ever since that word from the Lord. All you need is one word to see God do the miraculous, the undeniable, and the unbelievable.

I know that testimony may sound crazy, but sometimes you have to do something extreme and out of the ordinary. Now God may not tell you to go out on your front deck and yell at the top of your voice in the middle of the winter, but I can assure you that sometimes He'll take "the foolishness of the world to confound the wise." So, come on, get crazy, act like you have lost your mind, because in order to live, you must die to self. But don't do as I did. At least brush your hair before you go outside!

There will come a time in your life, if you haven't already been there, when God will bring you to a place where there is no one else around except you and Him. Your pastor won't be there; neither will your mother, your grandmother, or some intercessor in the church. He will lead you down a path where you will be forced to trust Him all by yourself. Maybe you're there right now.

The Bible declares, "We wrestle not against flesh and blood, but against principalities, against powers, against the rulers of the darkness of this world, against spiritual wickedness in high places" (Eph. 6:12). Sometimes we forget who the real enemy is. It is not your husband, your wife, a supervisor, your rebellious child, that sickness or disease, or any other lie the enemy would tell you. Peter identifies who your true enemy is: "Be sober, be vigilant; because your adversary the devil, as a roaring lion, walketh about, seeking whom he may devour" (1 Pet. 5:8). The devil is your real enemy. You need to know that he is after you and your stuff, not to just hurt, injure, or slow you down, but he is bent on destroying you.

You have authority to speak to that spirit of sickness and disease in your body, that spirit of rebellion in your teenager, that adultery that is looming over your marriage, that spirit of destruction that is trying to destroy your finances, your dreams, and your vision. God has given you that power in the name of Jesus. He wants you to move in violent faith.

On your journey of violent faith, God will put you in situations and scenarios where you will be presented with a small window of opportunity to see if you are going to respond with obedience and faith. It will be your choice whether to obey or to let it pass you by. I am fully convinced that God will always have a people that will listen and obey the first time, but He will always give us the opportunity to demonstrate our faith, love, and loyalty to Him first.

THE PRICE OF VIOLENT FAITH

Every person who has ever exercised violent faith has paid a price to achieve that level of faith.

When Abraham stood on the mountaintop with his son—his promise from God—tied up, holding a dagger up above his son's head, getting ready to offer him as a sacrifice to God in total obedience, it took faith to know that God would provide another sacrifice.

When Esther went into the king's chamber without permission, saying, "If I die, I die," all for the sake of her people, it took strength and faith to know that she would emerge victorious.

When Elijah killed all of Jezebel's prophets on Mt. Carmel after God had sent the fire, it took faith to know that God was on his side.

Peter took the hand of the crippled man and said, "Silver and gold have I none... [but] in the name of Jesus Christ of Nazareth rise up and walk" (Acts 3:6). It took violent faith to lift that man up, not knowing what would happen next.

Jacob wrestled with the angel, tumbling, tossing, holding on for dear life, even as his hip was disjointed, and telling him, "I will not let you go until you bless me."

It is funny to me to hear how people describe my ministry as I minister to the Lord. They say things such as "You are a singing warrior," or "You are God's secret weapon."

I appreciate the spirit in which most of these things are said, and, yes, I am a Native American. I am very proud of my heritage. So that might explain why they think it is a warrior thing, but it has nothing to do with my heritage. It does have everything to do with my faith, my walk, my story, my testimony, and the way that my family raised me to go after the things of God with a passion, a fire, and a relentless valor.

Because of that, I am often misunderstood. Even as a child I felt that as I sang and ministered to the Lord, there was something that was happening that was greater than what I could possibly comprehend. There was a prophecy that was spoken over me that said:

"The anointing that is upon you is unique. It is prophetic, it is Word-oriented, and it is declarative. People cannot even understand you because there is such a prophetic dimension to your ministry. Even you cannot understand the depth that you walk in with it. People don't even know and understand that when you are singing over their house, it is prophetic; you are literally declaring things in the heavens over them."

People have enjoyed the entertainment value, but they have missed the spiritual preparation that took place prior to that move of God before declaring what I hear in the spirit, preaching and singing prophetic songs.

My husband tells a testimony of when he had just finished the tenth grade in high school. He had gone to a Charismatic meeting at a church in his hometown. He was really seeking the face of the Lord at that time in his life and was desperately hungry for the baptism of the Holy Spirit.

After the message that night, he went forward to be baptized with the Holy Spirit. He was then taken to a room with other believers who were seeking an infilling. Well, God gloriously baptized him that night. But before he left, a man of God prophesied this: "You will be a part of a ministry that will be known around the world for dynamic anointed ministry, but the one who will know you the most will be Satan."

I can honestly and truly say, along with my husband, that there have been many times in the past fifteen years where we have had to face many oppositions from the hand of the enemy. There have been times when we have felt as if he were breathing down our necks, because of his tenacity in trying to destroy the anointing that God had imparted to our lives. We have seen ourselves rise with violent faith and declare, "Greater is he that is in [me], than he that is in the world" (1 John 4:4).

Violent faith is what I have found to be one of the secret weapons to the anointing that I flow in and also seeing prayer answered. Violent faith is allowing God to work through you in ways that you would not normally act in. It is forgetting who you are, whom you know, what you do, or what title you hold. All you know is you need answers, and nothing moves the heart of the Father like faith.

Violent faith will get you to the point where there is no more self-centeredness left. When you become desperate enough, you will do anything to see God move in a situation, especially if you have a word from God, because one word from God can change everything. If God speaks a word to you to do something, ask the Holy Spirit to reveal truth, clarity, and assurance that it is in fact God. Believe me, He will do it.

Sometimes you have to step out in faith. It won't always be easy, especially if it comes against your pride or is what you may feel is "crazy" or silly.

I love the boldness and faith of mighty men and women of God who came before us. Smith Wigglesworth wasn't exactly popular in his days. He was a mighty man of faith and power and was not known as a man who followed the creeds, culture, and beliefs of the religious people of his day.

I read of an incident when Wigglesworth was praying for the sick. There was one man who came in a wheelchair accompanied by his doctor.

He looked at the doctor and said, "What is wrong with him?"

The doctor replied, "He has stomach cancer, and he is dying."

He then turned to the man and told him to stand up and lift his hands. With that, the man stood on his feet very feeble and timidly lifted his hands. Wigglesworth proceeded to form a fist and punched the man in the stomach as hard as he could.

The man collapsed on the floor in front of him and the crowd. The doctor screamed, "Oh, my God; you've killed him."

Sure enough, the man was unconscious. Wigglesworth acted as if nothing had happened. He looked at the long line of people waiting to be ministered to and said, "Next." The man suddenly got up off the floor and started running around the building screaming, "I'm healed," and praising God at the top of his voice.

Take It by Force!

Take Back by Force Your Possessions

Violent faith will take you into a zone that not even your family, much less the world, will be able to understand. But who cares, as long as you get your miracle. You are a child of God, and all the things that the devil is trying to do in your life don't have to be tolerated. God has given you the power and the authority to take back by force what is rightfully yours.

We have to get out of fear and get into faith and realize, "Wait a minute, these are *my* children." Your children were not meant to be on drugs and alcohol, but they were meant to lay hands on the sick, cast out devils, and perform signs and wonders in the earth.

Tell the devil, "This is my marriage, my body, my finances, my dreams; you have no right." Stand strong in the Lord and in the power of His might, walk right up to the devil, and very emphatically tell him, "Give me back my stuff, because it belongs to me and it belongs to God. You have no right." Then stand back and see the salvation of the Lord as you take back by force your possessions and then begin to thank Him for the victory already won!

Does that mean you walk up to that husband who has been cheating on you and hit him upside the head, in the name of Jesus? No! I wouldn't advise that. However, I would tell you that in the supernatural world, through prayer, that is exactly what you can do to those demons that have been assigned to your marriage and family.

Violence in this text means "divine strength imparted by the Holy Spirit to get things accomplished in the supernatural that could never be done in the natural."

For instance, if you are living with a husband who is unsaved, you want more than anything to see him come to Jesus and to be the priest and the prophet of your house as God ordained it to be. So with "violent faith," as soon as he leaves the house, put on anointed worship music. Place anointed prayer cloths in his pillowcase or in his favorite chair, and pray in the Spirit, calling forth those things that are not as though they are.

52

In the natural, he may be unfaithful to you or he may be an alcoholic. But in the supernatural, he is the priest and prophet of your house.

When everyone else gives up on your husband, your wife, your children, your marriage, or your ministry, you will be the one left standing saying, "In the natural, I know it doesn't look good, but I am not walking in the natural. I am walking in the supernatural." The Bible says that the just shall live and walk by faith, and we don't walk by sight but by faith. "I know whom I have believed, and am persuaded that he is able to keep that which I have committed unto him" (2 Tim. 1:12).

One spring day while cleaning in my daughter's room I found a wasps' nest nestled between the outside of her window and the window screen. I could have easily have said, "Oh, look, isn't that interesting? I sure hope one of those wasps doesn't escape through the window and get my baby," or I could have said, "Oh, I'll have Jamie take a look at this when he gets home and see what he thinks." On the contrary; I immediately called my husband at our office and informed him of the intruders.

He rushed home and got the necessary things that he needed to rip away the wasps' nest. We were not about to play the wait-and-see game, because there was a danger lurking that could possibly harm our little girl. He totally annihilated the nest, the wasps, and even cleaned the area so there was not even a trace of them left.

That is exactly what needs to happen in so many homes in North America and around the world. The devil has come in and conveniently parked himself where he feels no one will see him. The Word says he parades himself as "an angel of light" (2 Cor. 11:14), but the Word also says, "We are not ignorant of his devices" (2 Cor. 2:11).

You don't play patty-cake with him, but you expose and violently destroy his plot, his plan, and his devices. Then you clean it all away with the washing of the Word and determine that your home will be a haven for your valuable possessions.

I'm talking about the kind of faith that will cover a son's bedroom with anointing oil while you are praying in the Spirit and calling forth things in the supernatural, even though in the natural you know it is a mess.

When you become extreme in your faith, everything changes. Your prayer life, a desire to fast, and a hunger for the things of God will increase. Praise and worship will be a part of your daily walk, and there will be a determination that nobody or nothing can shake.

Right now believe God for the impossible, and get ready to learn to walk in the power of violent faith.

And from the time John the Baptist began preaching and baptizing until now, *the kingdom of heaven has been forcefully advancing,* and violent people attack it.
—MATTHEW 11:12, NLT, EMPHASIS ADDED

Chapter Four

THE POWER OF MATTHEW 11:12

IN EVERY MAJOR battle, the army that wins the war marches into the heat of the battle with a strategy and determination. Part of winning the battle is having the mind-set of a victor.

When the Japanese attacked our men on our territory, we didn't just throw our arms up in defeat and surrender. We retaliated and took back control of what was rightfully ours in the first place. When terrorists tried to intimidate us on our own turf, we didn't shriek in cowardice. No. We forcefully advanced to seek out this cowardly enemy who hides behind its people and fanaticism.

So it is with the kingdom of God and the spirit realm. We need to learn what it means to "forcefully advance" and "violently attack" the kingdom of darkness. We need to move from victim mentality to victorious living.

THE FORERUNNER OF SPIRITUAL GUERRILLA WARFARE

We have an unseen enemy who does not believe in fighting fair. He is a thief, a liar, and a destroyer. He employs military guerilla tactics in this spiritual battle.

But in every major season on God's calendar, God has always raised up a mighty man or woman of God who has stood out as a forerunner of that season's inception. These men and women of God used the devil's own strategy against him to bring him down and forcefully advance the kingdom of God.

There were many warriors for God. For example:

- God instructed Noah to build the ark because a flood was coming.

- God called Abraham to be the father of many nations.

- God made Joseph prime minister in the land of his bondage.

- Moses became the leader of the children of Israel and led them out of Egypt.

- Joshua and Caleb brought the Israelites into the Promised Land.

- God raised up a mighty woman of God by the name of Deborah to become a judge over her people.

- Samuel was God's prophet who stood for righteousness in the middle of darkness.

- David was a man after God's own heart whose lineage was established forever.

- Esther saved her people from inevitable destruction.

- God sent the prophets Elijah, Elisha, and the judges to prophesy to His people the Word of the living God.

But the greatest forerunner of them all was John the Baptist. Jesus said of him:

> But what went ye out for to see? A prophet? yea, I say unto you, and more than a prophet. For this is he, of whom it is written, Behold, I send my messenger before thy face, which shall prepare thy way before thee. Verily I say unto you, Among them that are born of women there hath not risen a greater than John the Baptist: notwithstanding he that is least in the kingdom of heaven is greater than he.
>
> —MATTHEW 11:9–11

Dressed in camel's hair, a leather girdle about his loins, and feasting on locust and wild honey, John came declaring, "Repent ye: for the kingdom of heaven is at hand. For this is he that was spoken of by the prophet Esaias [Isaiah], saying, The voice of one crying in the wilderness, Prepare ye the way of the Lord, make his paths straight" (Matt. 3:2–3).

When John came on the scene, it was at the right time in history. He was the one to announce the coming of the long-awaited Messiah, and Jesus came in the fulfillment of His Father's plan. It was all in God's timing, to fulfill the purpose that the Father had destined before the world began. From the beginning of John's ministry, right up until his imprisonment by King Herod, God had used this man, in a violent fashion, to go against the norms of his day.

John the Baptist's "church" wasn't a beautiful sanctuary with padded pews. No. His "church" was in the middle of the wilderness. When it came time for baptizing new converts, they weren't baptized in a beautiful baptistery with nice, clean-flowing water. Rather, the baptistery was a muddy stream that he found and dipped his new converts into. He wasn't a scholar, and his speech wasn't very eloquent either. The first thing out of his mouth to the Pharisees and Sadducees who came to the baptism was: "O generation of vipers, who hath warned you to flee from the wrath to come?" (Matt. 3:7). John the Baptist was not a subtle man.

The kingdom of God had suffered violence, ridicule, and persecution from the hands of the Roman government, the Pharisees, and the religious scribes. They hated the way that John looked, they hated all the attention he was getting, and they certainly hated his message. Not only was he prophesying all the things that were about to take place, but he was also declaring and announcing the fulfillment of the Messiah's kingdom.

John rubbed the religious folk the wrong way. His philosophy went against the grain of the religious people, because Jesus wasn't anything like they expected their Messiah to be. Up until that time, all that the people had were Moses' laws and the prophets, which no one could successfully live by (Luke 16:16). But when John came along announcing the kingdom of God was here, everyone began to say, "If the Messiah is coming, I want to be a part of His kingdom. What do I have to do? Count me in."

Picture a world with political unrest, no stability, strife, sickness, disease, poverty, dishonesty, and corruption. Much like our world today, this was the way the world looked when Jesus came on the scene. Then John appears announcing, "Your long-awaited promise of redemption and help is here." You can imagine the joy, thrill, and excitement that everyone felt in hearing these words after praying for deliverance for hundreds of years.

Their long-awaited Messiah who would come and rule with power, avenge their enemies, and set up His kingdom was finally here. Everyone was pressing in because they wanted to be a part of this kingdom to which John was referring. One writer says, "The kingdom is pictured as a besieged city, with all classes of men hammering at it from the outside, trying to get in, but a certain spiritual violence is necessary."[1]

THE FORCEFULLY MARCHING ARMY

We are an army that is marching forth with truth in the Word of God, and our hearts are filled with faith. We are pursuing integrity, godly character, and balance, and we are taking our position and authority in the kingdom realm. We will not retreat, back down, or give up. We know our Commander in Chief has never steered us wrong, and while we are following Him, He will never lead us astray. We are fearless, faithful, firm, steadfast, unmovable, and always abounding in the work of the Lord, and we know that our labor (or our faith) is not in vain. (See 1 Corinthians 15:58.)

And from the time John the Baptist began preaching and baptizing *until now*—this present time or moment that you are in right now—the kingdom of heaven has been forcefully advancing, and *violent people* attack it. Eager multitudes have been pressing into it, and violent people take it by force. That is you and me!

When I speak of violent people, I am not referring to someone who is mean, vindictive, angry, abusive, or who behaves in an unorderly fashion. On the contrary, I'm referring to people who love God and who are people of faith. A person who has violent faith is someone who is aggressive with their faith, someone who will dare to believe God in spite of the way the circumstance looks, how bad things sound, or how awful he feels. People of violent faith are those who will dare to believe God despite their cultural background, their traditional religious rituals, or even their present environment.

When the Word of God speaks of the kingdom of God forcefully advancing, it is declaring this word not only in John's day, but in our day as well. This is the greatest day to be alive on the face of this planet. Never have we seen technology advance so quickly as we have seen in the last fifty years.

What we are seeing with our eyes are things that our parents and grandparents never dreamed of. Palm-size computers, the information superhighway, cell phones the size of a credit card, pagers, and satellites that reach around the world carrying the gospel to literally every tribe and nation. Medical advancements and thousands of inventions have changed the face of how we live in the world. They are a huge indication of the End Times. The Bible says that in the last days, "knowledge shall be increased" (Dan. 12:4).

In the same sense, the kingdom of God has seen advancement on a scale that is unprecedented also. Never have we seen revelation knowledge come forth from men and women of faith as we have seen over the last century.

- When God needed a man to cause a reformation who would preach a message of *justification*, He called Martin Luther.

- When God needed a man to proclaim *sanctification*, He called John Wesley.

- When God needed a *violent anointing* to come on the scene to demonstrate His power, a man fired up with the power of God, ready to take on any demon or devil of hell to get people saved, set free, delivered, and healed, He called Smith Wigglesworth.

And the kingdom of God kept advancing:

- When God wanted to use a woman who didn't care what anyone said but was willing to operate under such a violent anointing that people got up out of wheelchairs, He anointed Kathryn Kuhlman.

- When God needed a soulwinner who would carry this gospel of the Lord Jesus Christ from continent to continent, He anointed Dr. Billy Graham.[2]

- When God needed a man who would boldly proclaim that "Jesus is Lord" and preach the Word of faith with power and clarity, He called Kenneth Copeland.

- When God needed a mighty man who would break the record in the *Guinness Book of World Records* for bringing the largest group of families together to one city and then prophesy to them "thou art loosed," He called Bishop T. D. Jakes.

- When God needed a man of God to stand up and call a nation back to holiness and purity and to "raise the standard" and to be a "repairer and restorer," He called a tall, skinny preacher from the cornfields of Ohio by the name of Pastor Rod Parsley.

- When God needed a woman who would teach the practicality of living life with joy and teach the body of Christ that they can enjoy everyday life as they live for Jesus, He anointed Joyce Meyer.

- When God needed a woman who would operate in the office of a prophet to declare to her generation that God requires purity and holiness and a life that is "for real," He anointed Prophetess Juanita Bynum.

The list could go on and on for the mighty men and women of God that He has used to advance His kingdom for the saving of many souls.

MOVEMENTS THAT ADVANCED THE KINGDOM OF GOD

Just in the last century we have seen many great moves of God that have greatly affected where we are on God's calendar and timetable: the Pentecostal movement, the Healing Revival, the Charismatic movement, and so on. Please allow me to briefly touch on the Pentecostal movement and the Healing Revival in this chapter.

The Pentecostal movement brought many mighty men and women of God to the forefront to bring about change, not only in the church, but also in the society of their day. John Alexander Dowie, Maria Woodworth-Etter, Evan Roberts, William Seymour, John G. Lake, and Smith Wigglesworth.

The writer of Hebrews tells us:

> Remember your leaders, those who spoke to you the word of God; consider the outcome of their way of life, and imitate their faith.
>
> —HEBREWS 13:7, RSV

Just before he died, Smith Wigglesworth, one of the greatest spiritual leaders of this century, prophesied concerning a vision about revival. He said:

> I see it! I see a revival coming to planet earth as never before. There will be untold multitudes who will be saved. No man will say, "So many and so many," because no man will be able to count those who will come to Jesus Christ. I see it! The dead will be raised, the arthritic healed, cancer will be healed. No disease

will be able to stand before God's people, and it will spread all over the world. It will be a worldwide thrust of God's power and a thrust of God's anointing.[3]

I believe that what God showed this mighty man of God over fifty years ago is happening now on a worldwide scale.

If there was ever a time to seize this season of prophetic fulfillment and go after the things of God, to go after your unsaved loved ones, your health, your finances, your ministry, or whatever you are believing God for, now is the time. Don't wait. The kingdom of God is moving, and violent people attack it. Get in on it! Get into what God is doing in the earth *right now!*

If it is people who are hindering you, then cut those relationships. If it is a church that is stunting your growth and, more importantly, your faith, *move!* The kingdom of God is advancing, and violent people, who know their God and who want to see Him do the impossible, attack it. They go after their miracle with all diligence.

The power of Matthew 11:12 simply stated is this: the power of the resurrected Christ, who is alive, is active inside you and available to every believer. Jesus said, "I assure you, of all who have ever lived, none is greater than John the Baptist. Yet even the most insignificant person in the Kingdom of Heaven is greater than he is!" (Matt. 11:11, NLT). Jesus was saying that in view of the prophetic. Not only did He know the cross was ahead of Him and the awful price He would have to pay, but He also knew the glory, redemption, and victory it meant for every believer on the other side of the cross. On the other side of the cross, we would walk in power and authority that John the Baptist could only dream about. On the other side of the cross, we would be able, by the power of the Holy Spirit, to do "greater works" than even Jesus Himself, simply because of the price that the Savior paid on the cross (John 14:12).

I don't know what crisis you are facing this very minute, but there is one thing I do know: there is a way out. Violent faith and violent people attack it with unwavering perseverance and stamina! Let the kingdom of God forcefully advance in your life. Get active and declare that this thing will not happen. I stand in the gap with you right now and declare that today everything changes. A deep-rooted trust in the unfailing Word of the living God, the powerful name of Jesus, the prayer of agreement with people of like faith, like spirit, like destiny, and like anointing can change everything. Here is a plan of attack to overcome your situation.

BATTLE PLAN OF ATTACK

1. Get organized.

The only way to truly win this war that you are waging is to be organized. The Bible specifically details what our stance should be, not just during wartime, but always.

> Wherefore take unto you the whole armour of God, that ye may be able to withstand in the evil day, and having done all, to stand. Stand therefore, having your loins girt about with truth [speak the truth, walk in truth, live the truth, in love], and having on the breastplate of righteousness [right living, right thinking, right being]; and your feet shod with the preparation of the gospel of peace [let peace rule in your heart, mind, and life]; above all, taking the shield of faith [substance of things hoped for and evidence of things not seen], wherewith ye shall be able to quench all the fiery darts of the wicked. And take the helmet of salvation [keep repentance a part of your life every day and guard your thought life], and the sword of the spirit, which is the word of God [hide it in your heart]: Praying always with all prayer and supplication in the spirit [never stop praying].
> —EPHESIANS 6:13–18

Nothing is more powerful than prayer and fasting. As you begin to pray and fast, God will send forth His ministering angels to come and give you the strength to not only win this battle, but also to be more than a conqueror (Rom. 8:37).

Then, never underestimate the power of agreement between you and other believers, because the Word declares that one can chase a thousand, but two of us can put ten thousand to flight (Deut. 32:30).

Finally, never forget to use the name that God has given to every believer, not your favorite TV evangelist or your God-fearing grandma, but the name that is above every name, the name of Jesus. It is a name that even at the very mention of it, demons tremble, because they know there is power in His name and in His shed blood on the cross.

2. Plan your attack.

I'm sure you have heard the catch phrase "Every winner plans to win, and every loser never plans anything." Proverbs 16:1 says, "The preparations of the heart in man, and the answer of the tongue, is from the LORD." We need to be reminded that it is all in the Father's hands, and He always likes it when His children win, especially when they realize who their opponent is (Satan, the defeated foe). We will always come out a winner if we lay our plans in the Father's hands.

First, God wants us to "commit [our] work unto the LORD" (Prov. 16:3). That is a strong suggestion coming from a very wise king under the inspiration of the Holy Spirit, and then, here is the promise: "And your plans will succeed" (Prov. 16:3, NIV).

What is it that you need for God to do in your particular situation? Take the time to write it down on a piece of paper. Habakkuk 2:2 instructs us to "write the vision, and make it plain." Sometimes we need to be reminded of some things that God has said, and the only way for it to become clear for us is to write it down. Now the paper doesn't mean anything, but when we hold it up to the Father with unwavering perseverance and diligence, and bring it before the Lord every day, then God will answer, because He is bound to His Word. One thing that you can count on, if you don't have a plan to win, then most likely you won't.

When a runner is preparing his body for a marathon, he puts

himself through rigorous routines to shape, mold, and discipline himself to win the race. His one aim and goal is to win. So it is with us. Paul said, "Know ye not that they which run in a race run all, but one receiveth the prize? So run, that ye may obtain" (1 Cor 9:24). How do we do it? "Looking unto Jesus the author and finisher of our faith" (Heb. 12:2).

We have to have a plan and a strategy to meet the daily challenges to win back our stuff from the hand of the enemy, and here is how.

1. Find a quiet time every morning before your day begins to be alone with God in prayer and in His Word.

2. Before you leave that quiet place, spend time in worship and praise with your favorite cassette tape or CD.

3. Keep a prayer in your heart. The Bible says, "Pray without ceasing." There will need to be some adjustments made to your mind. Speak to yourself and say, "I have the mind of Christ."

3. Remember—timing is everything.

This is usually a very hard one for us because it requires so much patience, but that is probably what Father God is trying to develop in us in the first place—patience.

Solomon said, "To everything there is a season, and a time to every purpose under the heaven" (Eccles. 3:1). That means that there are going to be times when you want God to do something— yesterday. And all you keep hearing Him say is, "For you have need of patience that after you have done the will of God you might receive the promise." The "old folks" used to sing a song, and they had it right. It said, "He may not come when you want Him, but He's always right on time."

Trust God with the timing. He knows what He is doing. At the right time, in the right season, in the right circumstance, and at the right moment, He's going to come through for you; don't quit believing. James wrote, "Is your life full of difficulties and temptations? Then be happy, for when the way is rough, your patience has a chance to grow. So let it grow, and don't try to squirm out of your problems. For when your patience is finally in full bloom, then you will be ready for anything, strong in character, full and complete" (James 1:2–4, TLB).

I can tell you from experience that I know it to be a fact that "he always does exactly what he says. He carries out and fulfills all of God's promises, no matter how many of them there are" (2 Cor. 1:19–20, TLB).

Be determined that you are going to focus on the supernatural instead of the natural. Never quit trusting God for your miracle and believing that it shall come to pass. When you boldly claim the promises of God in faith, you reveal and unleash your authority.

But if the Spirit of him that raised up Jesus from the dead dwell in you, he that raised up Christ from the dead shall also quicken your mortal bodies by his Spirit that dwelleth in you.

—ROMANS 8:11

Chapter Five

AUTHORITY REVEALED AND UNLEASHED

HAVING GROWN UP as the "baby" in a family of twelve children, I was often times snubbed off with comments such as, "Oh, she's just the baby; she can't do it. Let one of her older sisters do it." I took to heart what people said about me. I felt inadequate in so many ways that I believed the image that people were painting of me. Consequently, I told myself that I would always be shy, backward, and would struggle with everything in life the way that I had struggled in school, just barely passing my grade. While one of my older sisters excelled with high honors in grade school, high school, and eventually college, I, on the other hand, had to seek help with every new endeavor that would come my way.

Although I had a wonderful family that encouraged me, I still listened and believed what some negative people around me thought and said about me. However, I had such a desire to have the anointing and presence of God in my life and to be mightily used by Him that I sought God and His best even from the beginning of my salvation experience at the early age of eight years old. Then when I turned twelve, something drastic happened. I was baptized with the Holy Spirit. For three days and nights, I had an experience with God that very few twelve-year-olds have. I couldn't speak in English those three days, and I now know that God was preparing me for my present journey.

I experienced such joy and enthusiasm about knowing God on a deeper level that it confused me to see so many people around me who were filled with the Holy Spirit as I was, but who were not experiencing the same joy and enthusiasm. Some people even said some things such as: "Don't go overboard now; you have to eat sometime, so don't get too spiritual." But they didn't understand. I wasn't physically hungry. Like Jesus, I was eating meat "that [they] knew not of" (John 4:32). They didn't understand that God had revealed and unleashed His authority in my life.

I am convinced the reason why so many people live such depressed, defeated lives is because they don't know who they are in Christ. Many people can't go on to maturity in the Lord because they lack authority. Without the Holy Spirit operating in your life, there is one thing that you can be assured of: you will never know true authority over Satan, sickness, poverty, or, quite frankly, anything else spiritually in your life.

AUTHORITY DEFINED

Webster's dictionary defines *authority* as "power to influence or command thought, opinion, or behavior; freedom granted by one in authority." The word *authorize* is also a very interesting word as we look at it in perspective to our redemption. It means "to invest especially with legal authority; to empower."

Have you ever been to a circus? I just love to go and see the clowns, the elephants, and trapeze artists. One of the most fascinating things to me, though, is when they bring out the lions and tigers. I have never seen them bring these huge cats out of their cages, only to see their trainer acting fearful. Picture a trainer coming into one of those cages, his face lined with fear, dancing around, running from one side to the other, trying his best to avoid these creatures. It wouldn't be something fascinating. It would be something very frightening to watch. You don't see these men and women cower in those cages, but rather, they step in with their whips, showing confidence and authority. Their shoulders are square, their heads are lifted up, and they are usually smiling, and, as a result, you see those mammoth animals, rise up, jump through fire, roll over, and obey any command given by the trainer.

That is the picture I want you to get every time you meet up with the forces of darkness. You don't step out into this arena called "life" and cower like a frightened little puppy. No, you stand strong in the power of His might. You don't have to crack a whip, but you do need to wield the Word of the living God, which is sharper than any two-edged sword. You declare the Word of the Lord to those forces of darkness that would devour your very life and watch them bow their knees to the authority that there is in the name of Jesus, all with the joy of the Lord on your face. *That is authority!*

AUTHORITY ENCOUNTERED

I remember in the early days of ministry when I was only a twelve-year-old youngster. I began to minister with my five older sisters. Those were very exciting times in my life, because it was great to be used by God and to see people saved, healed, and delivered.

The most interesting part to me was when someone got delivered from demonic possession; that always fascinated me. Although I was right there in the heat of the battle, I was not on the front battle lines, so to speak. My older siblings would handle that, and they were much more experienced and qualified with that than I was. After all, I was the "baby." I just stood up there, sang, and looked cute.

Interestingly enough, it was that very experience of demonic possession that the devil tried to use to intimidate me and to make me feel inadequate when I went out to minister as a soloist in my early days. I was grown up, a college graduate, and my family had all gone on with their lives. I was pursuing the call of God upon my life to preach, teach, and sing. I remember an incident when I was ministering in a church, and, all of a sudden, an anointing came into that building and brought such a deep conviction that sinners began to weep and literally run down to the altar to receive Jesus as their Lord.

Among this barrage of people running down the aisle was a young girl, maybe eighteen or nineteen years of age. She ran down and collapsed in front of the pulpit where I was ministering. She was crying so profusely that her cries turned into desperate sobs. I noticed her distinctly because she ran down and was trying to grab my feet. I had to literally back away to keep her from grabbing me.

All at once, her whole countenance changed, and she rose up and began shouting at the top of her voice, "I'm going to kill you! I'm going to kill you! I'm going to get you!" It was at this point that four very large, strong men grabbed this young girl, two on each arm. It was everything that they could physically do to try and keep her from me.

As she was spitting at me, I must confess, I was very shaken that this sort of thing was happening. For a split second, I had one of two choices. I could look around and see if there was a back door (which, to be honest, was the first impression that came to my mind), or I could look this demonic spirit in the face and tell him, "I am not running or leaving; I am not intimidated by you. You are the one who is leaving. I have authority over you in the name of Jesus." I quickly regained my composure and called the church to prayer.

(Sometimes when those situations arise, hopefully you have an opportunity to take the person to a private place, away from the view of the congregation so that he or she is not on public display, that is, if you get that chance. Other times you have to deal with that spirit immediately and in the open. Satan's plan is to disrupt anything that God is doing and to make spectacles of people.)

We began to call on the name of the Lord and to plead the blood of Jesus with authority over this girl's life. Not only was she saved that night, but she was also filled with the Holy Spirit. Later I talked with her and found out that she had been a backslider who was very much involved in witchcraft and the occult and was obsessed with heavy rock music.

AUTHORITY REVEALED

Did you know that the devil is afraid of you? With the power of the Holy Ghost upon you, he is afraid of you. The Bible declares, "Greater is he that is in you, than he that is in the world" (1 John 4:4).

We destroy satanic forces in our lives by quoting the Word. When we open our mouths and say: "It is written..." or "Devil, the Bible says...," we are experiencing the same authority that Jesus used in the wilderness when He was tempted. A lot of us can quote what someone else says, but not what the Bible says. I can promise you that what someone else says does not impress (or rebuke) the devil.

A great example of this during the early church is found in the Book of Acts. Seven Jewish men, the sons of a high priest named Sceva, had heard about the miracles that followed the apostle Paul's ministry, and they tried to imitate what Paul was doing. The problem was that they were not walking in God-given authority; they were walking in their own flesh.

> Then certain of the vagabond Jews, exorcists, took upon them to call over them which had evil spirits the name of the Lord Jesus, saying, We adjure you by Jesus whom Paul preacheth. And there were seven sons of one Sceva, a Jew, and chief of the priests, which did so. And the evil spirit answered and said, Jesus I know, and Paul I know; but who are ye? And the man in whom the evil spirit was leaped on them, and overcame them, and prevailed against them, so that they fled out of that house naked and wounded. And this was known to all the Jews and Greeks also dwelling at Ephesus; and fear fell on them all, and the name of the Lord Jesus was magnified. And many that believed came, and confessed, and shewed their deeds.
>
> —ACTS 19:13–18

These men learned a hard lesson fast.

You don't claim to do anything in Jesus' name just because someone else said it a certain way or said to do it. You walk in God-given authority because you know who you are in the Lord and His Word is on the inside of you so that when you face that demon, the only thing to come out of your mouth is the Word.

So the next time you meet up with opposition, sickness, or

temptation, don't say, "Devil, my grandma said..." or "My pastor told me..." or "My daddy told me to always remember...." If you do, he will stand there and laugh at you. But do say, "It is written..." or "The Bible says...," and watch him take off like a flash. Remember what the Bible says:

> For the word of God is quick, and powerful, and sharper than any twoedged sword, piercing even to the dividing asunder of soul and spirit.
>
> —Hebrews 4:12

The devil doesn't want you to possess your right as a child of God, because if you ever realize the power that you have over him through what Jesus did on the cross, he knows it annihilates his agenda "to steal, and to kill, and to destroy" (John 10:10). As the seed of Abraham and His heir and a joint heir with Jesus, God has given us the right to take back those possessions that belong to us. He wants us to walk in the authority that He has given us.

The Bible declares, "Greater works than these shall [you] do; because I go unto my Father" (John 14:12). What kind of works was Jesus doing when He was on the earth? He was healing the sick, casting out demons, raising the dead, setting people free, and getting them delivered. These were the things that He was doing, and yet, Jesus said we would do greater works than these. Those greater works don't come about because we think we are "all that," but they come as a result of intimacy and relationship with the One to whom all power belongs.

It doesn't matter if you are male, female, black, white, Hispanic, Oriental, fat, skinny, educated, or completely illiterate. If you say the name of Jesus, you have the authority that Jesus said was yours through His name. This means you are victorious in every situation no matter what it may seem like, and you have every right as His child to have everything you need to be an overcomer. Jesus came to "destroy the works of the devil" (1 John 3:8), and that is your mission as part of the church—to destroy the devil's works, schemes, and plans.

We must fight for our inheritance. It is ours, and we must remind the devil that it is our names that appear in the Lamb's Book of Life, not his! He has already blown his opportunity. The problem is that many believers today don't know how to fight. They would rather flee than fight. But it is time to put him on the run for a change.

At some time in your walk with the Lord as you seek to go up and reclaim territory that is rightfully yours, you are going to face some opposition. You had better decide now whether you are going to run or stand flat-footed and say, "I *will* stand!" Then put the devil on the run by declaring who you are in Christ.

That night in the service when the demon-possessed teenager tried to attack me, I realized that I was no longer cute, little Judy. God had given me power and authority through Jesus Christ to minister deliverance to that girl, and the devil wasn't going to humiliate me and make a mockery of God's almighty power.

If I had called the pastor to come and to take over the service and cowered in the back corner, the devil would have taken that opportunity, and many others, to tell me, "See there; I told you that you weren't called to the ministry. This is too hard for you; give up before I really do kill you." But I didn't listen. Instead, I put *him* on the run, and deliverance from demonic possession is still a vital part of my ministry today.

I love it when the Word declares that the same power "that raised up Christ from the dead…shall also quicken your mortal bodies" (Rom. 8:11). That means the very same power that got Jesus out of the grave is in you. Not in your favorite evangelist or pastor, but *in you*.

When Jesus looked up into the heavens and declared, "It is finished!", all of hell began a party. Can you imagine the devil and all his demons feeling so victorious and everyone dancing around, giving each other high fives? Then all of a sudden all of hell began to tremble as the dead Savior became the living Conqueror. Jesus stepped into the corridors of the dead and the damned, walked up to a trembling Satan, and said to him, "Give Me the keys. I want the keys to death, hell, and the grave." At that moment Satan didn't have a choice; he handed over the keys. Jesus said, "No more can you hold My people in bondage. They are free from your chains." The Bible declares that Christ returned triumphantly from heaven after His resurrection and triumphed over Satan. "He led captivity captive, and gave gifts unto men" (Eph. 4:8), indicating Satan's ultimate defeat in the heavenlies, in the earth, and under the earth.

Jesus arose from the dead defeating all the power of the devil. If Satan had known that Jesus would defeat him, he would have never crucified the Lord of glory. (See 1 Corinthians 2:8.) But that's what the devil gets for being stupid, because anybody who tries to over-throw God is pretty stupid.

I remember a powerful testimony from a pastor friend of ours from Florida who pastors an inner-city church. Gang members began harassing the parishioners and the community so much to the point that someone was killed in a drive-by shooting. The pastor was obviously very concerned for his parishioners and community, so he called a forty-day fast.

In the middle of the fast, the pastor's secretary walked into his office. Pale with fright, she started stuttering the dreadful news. "P-P-Pastor, they're here!"

"Who's here?" he said.

"The gang members," she replied, "and they have brought their leader with them. They say they're not leaving until they see you."

The pastor said that, for a moment, fear crept in, but then, like a mighty wind, the Spirit of God rushed upon him with a peace that could not be explained, and then he felt an overwhelming sense of calmness.

He said to his secretary, "Send them in."

They came in, one by one with their spiked, multicolored hair, body piercings, and tattoos of every size, color, shape, and disgusting displays. The leader was the last one to enter, and he came in with a vengeance.

The pastor's first thought was to try and bring a sense of calmness to this meeting, so he invited them to have a seat. It was then that the leader spoke up and began shouting obscenities at the pastor, telling him, "I didn't come here today to sit down and rap with you. I came here today to tell you that you are through in this city. This city belongs to me, and you are finished. It is time for you to go."

The pastor said he could see the demonic oppression on this young man's face and could sense the awful grip of satanic powers in his life. The pastor, with power, authority, and boldness, interrupted the young man and said, "Well, son, let me tell you what God just told me to tell you. God said if you don't repent in the next thirty seconds, you're going to be dead."

"You're not scaring me with that religion stuff," he said. "I'm telling you, your time is up."

"OK," the pastor said, "but you have twenty seconds left." All the while the pastor kept observing his watch while the other gang members became restless and fidgety, saying, "Come on, man. Let's get out of here. I don't like what I'm feeling."

The gang leader replied, "No one is moving. He's trying to bluff us."

The pastor, looking at his clock, said, "you have 10...9...8..."

The young man responded, "Stop it, man. I don't like that."

The pastor ignored his plea and continued the countdown, "7...6...5..."

"Come on, man, quit it."

"4...3..."

All of a sudden, the leader fell down on his knees and began to cry out, "O God, dear Jesus, I'm sorry, Lord. Please come into my heart, Lord; forgive me, Jesus."

Right there the entire gang gave their hearts to Jesus, and revival broke out in the church and in the community.

The pastor told me, "I would have never said that unless the Holy Spirit directed me to say it."

That is an example of how the authority of God will rise within us when we don't know what to do. Jesus said, "I give unto you power to tread on serpents and scorpions, and over all the power of the enemy" (Luke 10:19). We have authority and power over *all* the power of Satan, and it's time we use it.

AUTHORITY EXPOSED

I believe one of the reasons why so many Christians are being robbed and living such defeated, depressed, and unfulfilled lives in God's kingdom is because they don't understand who they are in Christ. Let's see who the Word declares you to be.

You are an heir of God and joint heir with Christ.

> The Spirit itself beareth witness with our spirit, that we are the children of God: and if children then heirs; heirs of God, and joint-heirs with Christ.
>
> —ROMANS 8:16–17

You are the anointed one.

> The Spirit of the Lord GOD is upon me; because the LORD hath anointed me to preach good tidings unto the meek; he hath sent me to bind up the brokenhearted, to proclaim liberty to the captives, and the opening of the prison to them that are bound; to proclaim the acceptable year of the LORD, and the day of vengeance of our God; to comfort all that mourn; to appoint unto them that mourn in Zion, to give unto them beauty for ashes, the oil of joy for mourning, the garment of praise for the spirit of heaviness; that they might be called trees of righteousness, the planting of the LORD, that he might be glorified.
>
> —ISAIAH 61:1–3

You are chosen.

For you are a chosen people. You are a kingdom of priests, God's holy nation, his very own possession. This is so you can show others the goodness of God, for he called you out of the darkness into his wonderful light.

—1 PETER 2:9, NLT

You are His glorious church.

That he might sanctify and cleanse it with the washing of the water by the word, that he might present it to himself a glorious church, not having spot, or wrinkle, or any such thing.

—EPHESIANS 5:26–27

You are the redeemed.

Forasmuch as ye know that ye were not redeemed with corruptible things, as silver or gold, from your vain conversation . . . but with the precious blood of Christ, as of a lamb without blemish and without spot.

—1 PETER 1:18–19

You have authority and power.

Behold, I have given you authority to tread on serpents and scorpions, and over all the power of the enemy.

—LUKE 10:19, NAS

You have a destiny.

"For I know the plans I have for you," declares the LORD, "plans to prosper you and not to harm you, plans to give you hope and a future."

—JEREMIAH 29:11, NIV

Yes! We are heirs, and we are the anointed! We are the chosen, and we are His glorious church. We are the redeemed, and we most certainly have authority and power that have been given to every heir of God and joint heir with Christ. Thank God we do have destiny!

So then why do we listen to the lies?

Don't just stand there. Open your mouth and speak life back into that situation. Life and death are in the power of the tongue (Prov. 18:21).

When the enemy says to you, "You are a loser," you should declare to his face, "No, stupid, you are the loser. You are the one who will spend eternity in the fire. I'm a winner, because Paul said, 'Now thanks be unto God, which always causeth us to triumph in Christ...' (2 Cor. 2:14). The Greater One is inside of me. It is impossible for me to be a loser."

When he whispers in your ear, "Hey, you sure are depressed today. This is going to be an awful day. You should stay in bed today and not get up," it is then that you should get up from where you are and say, "Oh, no, devil! I am an overcomer. Romans 8:37 says, 'Overwhelming victory is [mine] through Christ who loved [me] enough to die for [me]' (TLB). And besides that, 'I can do everything God asks me to with the help of Christ who gives me the strength and power' (Phil. 4:13, TLB). I declare that I am 'the head and not the tail, and [I] shall always have the upper hand' (Deut. 28:13, TLB). I not only swim in the water, praise God, I walk on the water. 'No weapon turned against [me] shall succeed, and [I] will have justice against every...lie' (Isa. 54:17, TLB)."

Let a song of praise flow from your lips: "I will bless the LORD at all times: his praise shall continually be in my mouth" (Ps. 34:1).

The devil says, "You are sick and can't get well, and you know what the report and what the doctor said." Yes, you may know the *facts*, but the *truth* is, "He was wounded for our transgressions, he was bruised for our iniquities: the chastisement of our peace was upon him; and with his stripes we are healed" (Isa. 53:5). Begin to declare aloud:

- I have authority over this sickness and disease in my body. I only have to speak the Word of faith. It is even now in my mouth. I pull down fear because God has not given me a spirit of fear, but of power, of love, and a sound mind. (See 2 Timothy 1:7.)

- I have complete control over my mind because "[I cast] down imaginations, and every high thing that exalteth itself against the knowledge of God, and [bring] into captivity every thought to the obedience of Christ" (2 Cor. 10:5).

Understand that you have authority and power in the name of Jesus through the infallible Word of God.

I don't have to worry whether or not my children will be saved, because the Word has already covered it. "Believe in the Lord Jesus, and you will be saved—you and your household" (Acts 16:31, NIV).

I don't have to be concerned about whether or not I am going to be provided for in the future, because He gave me His Word:

If God so clothe the grass of the field, which to day is, and to morrow is cast into the oven, shall he not much more clothe you?

—MATTHEW 6:30

You don't have to fear or dread terror or any other calamity that is threatening, for "he that dwelleth in the secret place of the most High shall abide under the shadow of the Almighty" (Ps. 91:1).

A man (or woman) of God will never rise above what he believes is his self-image. If you listen to negative thoughts in your mind and fellowship with pessimistic people who are always telling you what you *can't* do, then you will never see the fulfillment of God's plan and purpose for your life. It is not so much who *people* say and think you are as it is whom *God* says and thinks you are.

AUTHORITY UNLEASHED

I once received an e-mail from a lady who experienced authority unleashed firsthand. While traveling in a plane thirty thousand feet in the air, the plane's cabin suddenly began to fill with smoke. The flight attendants started running around, feverishly giving everyone instructions. The plane began to do a semi-nose dive, and as she held her head down, suddenly her life flashed before her. She saw her husband, children, and grandchildren, and she thought to herself, *O God, this is it. I'm going to die!*

All of a sudden, like a flash, she was reminded of the word of God that she had received at one of our meetings: "There is a greater boldness, a new authority, and an aggressiveness in the spirit realm that is coming to you." She was reminded of the verse, "The same power that raised Jesus from the dead is inside you. I will give you power over all the enemy." She realized that the devil was trying to take her out, so she said she screamed as loud as she could, "I shall not die, but live, and declare the works of the LORD" (Ps. 118:17).

With that, she screamed as loud as she could, "Is there anybody on this plane full of the Holy Ghost?"

She said there was one man in the back that screamed, "Yes, I'm full of the Holy Ghost."

She said, "Sir, will you agree with me that we are going to take authority over this plane in the name of Jesus?"

He shouted back, "Yes, I will agree with you."

If you are going through a crisis, then find one more believer to agree with you. Jesus said, "If any two of you shall agree on earth as touching any thing that they shall ask, it shall be done for them of my Father" (Matt. 18:19). If you can't find someone to agree with you, then ask the Holy Spirit to agree with you, and He will.

She then declared, "In the name of Jesus, plane, I command you to operate and function in the way that you were created to operate and function, and you will land us safely." All of a sudden the plane began to lift back up to its normal place, and they landed safely.

That authority and power is in you, so use it whether you're on a plane, in your house, on the job, on your sick bed, or wherever the opportunity presents itself. You may find yourself facing a situation like I had to face with the young girl in one of my services. Maybe you feel like you would love to find a back door and escape because you're fighting the very demons of hell. Let me remind you: *you and God are the majority.*

When the armies with their horses and chariots were coming against Elisha and his servant, the servant said to Elisha, "'Alas, my master! What shall we do?' So he answered, 'Do not fear, for those who are with us are more than those who are with them.' Then Elisha prayed and said, 'O LORD, I pray, open his eyes that he may see.' And the LORD opened the servant's eyes, and he saw; and behold, the mountain was full of horses and chariots of fire all around Elisha" (2 Kings 6:15–17, NAS).

Whatever you do, don't run. Stay and fight for what is rightfully yours. Get up right now off of your sofa or your chair, get your hands in the air, open your mouth, and begin to declare boldly who you are in Christ. Get some praise on your lips, and then watch God be God.

You're not by yourself. Plead the blood over that situation, speak the name of Jesus, speak forth life and the Word, and command your eyes to be opened to see the host of angels with holy fire surrounding you ready to do battle. Then, by all means, square your shoulders and lift up your head, because the Lion of the tribe of Judah is in control. You know who you are in Christ. Don't just take it. Take back what's yours, for there is a cause!

And David said...Is there not a cause?

—1 Samuel 17:29

Then as I looked over the situation, I called together the leaders and the people and said to them, "Don't be afraid! Remember the Lord who is great and glorious! *Fight for your friends, your families, and your homes."*

—Nehemiah 4:14, TLB, emphasis added

Thus saith the Lord; Refrain thy voice from weeping, and thine eyes from tears: for thy work shall be rewarded, saith the Lord; and they shall come again from the land of the enemy. And there is hope in thine end, saith the Lord, that *thy children shall come again to their own border.*

—Jeremiah 31:16–17, emphasis added

Chapter Six

IS THERE NOT A CAUSE?

WEARY AND HUNGRY, the 507th Maintenance Company of the Army's Third Infantry Division took a wrong turn onto Highway 7 instead of Highway 1. What happened next can only be described as a nightmare to those who lived to see its tragic end. Surrounded by their Iraqi attackers, the convoy came under heavy enemy fire.

One young girl in particular, Pfc. Jessica Lynch, was caught in the crossfire with Iraqi militants. The command was given: "Lock and load," but as Private Lynch shot, her weapon jammed. She and several other soldiers were taken hostage to Saddam Hussein Hospital. Some of the soldiers from her platoon were severely injured, some were captured and tortured, while still others paid the ultimate price.

This young soldier from Palestine, West Virginia, seized all of our hearts, and we felt for the first time how very repulsive war can become.

People began to question even the very existence of allowing women to be in the military. These women were our mothers, our daughters, our sisters, and our friends. *How could we face seeing these horrible images of brutal torture on our television screen? What could be done? Was there a way that we could get them back, and if so, what would be the cost of such a feat? Would it be worth risking the possibility of losing even more lives?* There had been many who had been captured and died at the hands of their captors in past wars, so what made this situation any different?

In the early morning hours of April 1, 2003, commandos raided Saddam Hussein Hospital and found Lynch: "Jessica Lynch, we're

American soldiers; we're here to take you home." Lynch replied, "I'm an American soldier, too."[1] For the American people, Lynch's rescue was a joyous moment in one of the darkest hours of Operation Iraqi Freedom.

But Jessica Lynch refuses to take credit for any heroics. For her, the true heroes are the soldiers who rescued her, those who were willing to risk their own lives for the sake of the cause: "Leave no man (or woman) behind."

The cause was for every person who died in the Twin Towers, at the Pentagon, and in a Pennsylvania field at the hands of some scheming, cowardly, and repulsive terrorists.

The cause was a nineteen-year-old girl who had been seriously injured in enemy crossfire, ultimately was captured, and was being held as a POW in a very hostile environment.

The cause was for every mother and father whose son or daughter had died in that awful raid to be a part of something that was greater than themselves.

The cause was for every American soldier of Operation Iraqi Freedom who had died.

The cause was for the high cost of *freedom*.

In the spiritual battle that you live out daily, *there is a cause*.

A WORTHY CAUSE

Webster's dictionary defines *cause* as, "a reason or motive for some action."

I would say to you right now that there is a cause for your violent faith. There is a reason why you must stand firm in the face of opposition.

The cause is so that you can enjoy life as God intended for every one of His children to live it—*abundantly*. Not in sickness or disease, or living out your days dreading every moment, but live it to its fullest potential.

The cause is to live in a fulfilled marriage where the union between a man and a woman is exactly as God purposed for it to be—for the husband to love his wife as Christ loves the church; for the woman to honor, cherish, and respect her husband in the same manner; and for the two to be one.

The cause is to see your son or daughter become the man or woman of God that he or she was destined to be before the world began; to see them walk in the divine purposes of God Himself; to live a life pleasing unto the Father; and, ultimately, to bring glory to His name and His kingdom.

The cause is to walk in prosperity and blessings laid down by the covenant that God gave to Abraham, and to walk in a manner where you are blessed to be a blessing to the nations and to finance the kingdom of God.

The cause is to see the plan and purposes of God come to pass in your life and in your ministry amid scorn, turbulent times, difficult decisions, and public opinion, and no matter what comes your way, to be determined to have all that God said that you could have.

There is a cause!

The devil would tell you to quit and stop believing because it is not worth it. But the devil is a liar, and he wants to stop you from coming into the greatness that the Father has promised to you as a believer.

DAVID'S CAUSE

Saul had lost the kingdom because of disobedience, and Samuel told Saul that God had rejected him as king and had given the kingdom to someone who was better than him. (See 1 Samuel 15:28.) In the meantime, Samuel had to figure out a way to get to Jesse's house to anoint one of his sons without Saul learning of it, because if Saul found out about Samuel anointing a new king, Samuel would be dead. Seven of Jesse's sons were presented before Samuel, and God rejected them all. Then Samuel asked, "Are these all the sons that you have?" Then Jesse remembered that his youngest, his "baby boy," was out in the fields tending sheep, and Samuel insisted on seeing him. When he appeared, the Bible says, "He was a fine-looking boy, ruddy-faced, and with pleasant eyes. And the Lord said, 'This is the one; anoint him'" (1 Sam. 16:12, TLB).

The rest, as they say, is history. David was anointed king of Israel. One day, Jesse sent David to take some roasted grain and loaves of bread to his brothers who were fighting the Philistines. When he arrived, he saw all the commotion on the battlefield and was especially drawn to the ten-foot giant who was screaming out curses to the army of Israel. David's response was, "Who is this heathen Philistine, anyway, that he is allowed to defy the armies of the living God?" (1 Sam. 17:26, TLB).

Immediately David's older brother reprimanded him, scorning him for being nosey and leaving his sheep unattended. Then David asked a very valiant question; he said, "*Is there not a cause?*" (1 Sam. 17:29, emphasis added). In other words, are we going to stand for this? Are we just going to continue to let this heathen curse our God? Is there not a cause to go after him? Is there not a reason to silence him? Yes, there is a cause because, ultimately, it is God's name and reputation that are at stake. Goliath is defying the armies of the living God, and David must defend the honor of the name of Jehovah God Almighty. In David's eyes, he was speaking about the One of whom he sang so sweetly so many times; he was referring to the One of whom David declared, "The LORD is my shepherd, I shall not want.... Thou preparest a table before me in the presence of mine enemies: thou anointest my head with oil.... Surely goodness and mercy shall follow me all the days of my life" (Ps. 23:1, 5–6). This was personal to him. Goliath was cursing the very One whom his "heart panteth after." David was filled with righteous indignation.

My friend, at some point you have to come to those same terms and say, "That's enough!", because it is Almighty God's name that is at stake—the very One you trust, the very One in whom you have put your confidence. You have put your whole heart and trust in what He has said to you through His Word and His servants. *There is a cause* because your God will keep that which you have committed to Him against that day. There is a cause, because your children are coming again to their own border (Jer. 31:17). There is a cause for fasting and praying, for Isaiah 58:8–9 declares, "If you do these things [fast], God will shed his own glorious light upon you. He will heal you.... Then when you call, the Lord will answer, 'Yes, I am here'" (TLB). He will quickly reply! Yes, there is a cause, and that cause is for everything that you are believing God to do.

NEHEMIAH'S CAUSE

Nehemiah was a great man of prayer and faith. He believed in the great God Jehovah who could answer prayer, so he prayed and travailed for the people of Israel to come back to their true and living God. He had heard about his people's plight and was in great distress over all the horrible things that were happening to them in Jerusalem. As the king's cupbearer, things were quite good for Nehemiah. But he was troubled because the city of Jerusalem was no longer powerful and beautiful, and its enemies were set on destroying its foundation. When he heard how the walls were broken down and the city was practically in ruins, he became deeply disturbed.

In essence, we are a lot like Nehemiah: enjoying life as we merrily go along, and then comes the phone call, the e-mail, or learning that someone very dear to us is in trouble and feeling the heaviness of that moment.

Nehemiah felt the call and the burden to go to the rescue of his people. As he went before the king with fear and trepidation, not knowing what the outcome would be when he would ask to be relieved of his duty, God granted him tremendous favor with King Artaxerxes. So the king sent him off with a host of the palace people to accompany him to his destination. He went to rebuild the walls, but when he got there, he met up with great opposition.

As I have said before, *there will always be an opposition to your mission.* If you have your mind set on following hard after God, whether it's going to the next level, believing for a miracle, or walking in violent faith, you will fight opposition most of the time.

I remember attending a service at Bishop T. D. Jakes' church shortly after he had moved into his beautiful sanctuary in Dallas, Texas. That night Bishop Jakes got up to greet the people and said in a cynical voice, "Well, we have had some strange things just show up on the front steps of our door just recently, left there by an apparent witch or some Satan worshipers in the area. My response is, 'What took you so long? I was about to think that you didn't know I was here.'"

Jesus said, "If the world hates you, you know that it hated Me before it hated you" (John 15:18, NKJV). When you are persecuted for Christ's sake, God will bless you and His glory will rest upon you. (See Matthew 5:11–12.) I don't know about you, but I want all the glory in my life that Father God has measured out for me.

Nehemiah's opposition was Sanballat the Horonite and Tobiah the Ammonite. They were determined to make sure that Jerusalem did not rise again to be the powerful and strong force that she was before the exile. So while Nehemiah and the other workers worked on the wall, Sanballat and Tobiah taunted, laughed, and threatened them to the point where the workers were intimidated and in fear for their very lives. But Nehemiah encouraged the people to ignore what was being said, and then he replied with this word from the Lord:

> Don't be afraid. Remember, the Lord who is great and glorious.
> —NEHEMIAH 4:14, TLB

When you keep the greatness of the Lord before you and think about who God is and how powerful He is, then there is no fear of what the enemy can do to you. Jesus said, "Do not be afraid of those who kill the body and after that can do no more. But I will show you whom you should fear: Fear him who, after the killing of the body, has power to throw you into hell" (Luke 12:4–5, NIV). Satan has no power over our lives. God has the ultimate say so.

Then Nehemiah tells them, "*Fight for your friends, your families, and your homes*" (Neh. 4:14, TLB, emphasis added).

That is the same reason why *you* must fight. What greater motivation do you need than that! If you can get a picture in your mind of what you are fighting for, then it will be a "good fight."

We have all heard incredible stories of a parent or a loved one performing tremendous feats of physical strength in the midst of a life-threatening situation. When the adrenaline starts flowing, the body's "fight or flight" response takes over. Some people have literally picked up cars or very heavy equipment to free a loved one. Moms and dads have been known to run through a burning house with debris falling all around them just to save their child from death. That is the kind of fight that I am talking about: a fight beyond human strength and human capability, the fight of faith and hope. Jude describes it as "[saving] some by snatching them from the very flames of hell itself" (Jude 23, TLB).

Announce to all the demons in hell, "You will not have my life, my family, this situation, because Jesus disarmed you and made a public example of you, triumphing over you." (See Colossians 2:15, RSV.)

GODLY SEED *IS* OUR CAUSE

If you are a parent, your godly seed is your cause regardless of how old your children may be. It is not too late to fight the good fight of faith and reclaim your children for His kingdom.

Most of us are familiar with Proverbs 22:6: "Train up a child in the way he should go: and when he is old, he will not depart from it."

Anne Gimenez wrote a powerful book titled *Marking Your Children for God.* In it she concludes:

> As I read [this scripture], it occurred to me: Solomon is talking about faith for my child's *future!*

Suddenly, I saw a gaping hole in my faith as a parent. I, like so many others, thought I was suppose to nurture my child carefully until she became a teenager. Then, just when she was hit with huge choices—about faith, her lifestyle, her friends and future—John and I were supposed to remove our hands....

But that's the moment she would need us most, when she would face all the attractions of the world. How we had been brainwashed!

Friends, with all the evil that is bombarding our children we need to do more than grab on to a verse about *future-tense faith*!...God is unveiling a powerful plan right now for our sons and daughters. And we as Christian parents need not sit idly by, adopting the hands-off attitude of the world, and allow them to be snatched away,...we must be mothers and fathers active rather than passive, and direct rather than indirect, in shaping the character of our children.[2]

As a parent, the greatest cause I have is to fight for my girls' future. I *am not* going to passively lie down and wait for the enemy to snatch them from me. No way!

One night while I was preaching this message on Matthew 11:12, a little boy about eight years old came to the altar. Many of those who came to the altar that night had needs, but I was especially drawn to this little guy, who was one of the first ones to come to the altar. When he came up, he wasn't looking around as someone his age would do, but he was earnestly seeking and crying out to the Lord as tears rolled down his cute, little face. His sincerity and genuine, earnest prayer touched my heart.

I walked over to where he was standing, and as I got closer, I could see a very concerned elderly couple standing behind him, which I later learned were his grandparents. I put my hand on the boy's shoulder and asked him if there was anything that I could help him pray about.

He looked up at me, quite surprised, to see me standing there, and with tears running down his cheeks he said, "Yes, ma'am. It's my daddy. I miss my daddy."

I said, "Where is your daddy?"

"My mommy and daddy are separated," he said, "and they are about to get a divorce, and I don't want that to happen because I would never get to see my dad. Who will play with me? Who will take me to my ball games?"

My heart went out to this child as I heard this story told through his eyes. Then this child said something to me that I will never forget. I saw a look of faith and determination on his face unlike anything I had seen on a child so young. It really astounded me. He said to me, "I heard you talking about violent faith, and that's what I want to do. I want to take my daddy back." It was so exciting to me to witness an eight-year-old boy actually get this message!

I took that little guy by the hand, and I said to him, "John,* do you believe the Bible is true?"

"Oh, yes, ma'am. I believe the Bible is God's Word," he responded.

I said, "The Bible says in Matthew 18:19, 'If two of you agree down here on earth concerning anything you ask for, my Father in heaven will do it for you'" (TLB).

I continued, "Will you agree with me that your mommy and daddy are going to get back together and that your daddy is going to come home?"

With even more excitement on his face, he gave me several quick nods of the head and responded very enthusiastically, "Yes, ma'am! Yes, ma'am!"

I prayed a very short, simple prayer asking God for those very things, and then we began to praise God for the answer to John's prayer, and that was it. I can tell you that I was delightfully blessed when I received a letter about two weeks later from John's mother letting me know that God had granted John's request. She and her husband, John's father, were back together and in church again. How thrilling! God is so good, and He still answers prayer.

---

*Fictitious name

LEAVING A LEGACY IS REASON FOR THE CAUSE

The Bible declares in Isaiah 8:18 that our "children are...for signs and for wonders." God wants to release miracles in our children as we yield them for His glory. God wants to bring forth godly seed through us. (See Malachi 2:15.) That godly seed is our children, our heritage, our legacy.

God can use a child to bring hope to a hopeless situation or a young person to give you strength for what you are going through. God is using young people as never before. There is a boldness and an authority in their spirits that is really striking. I see it even in my five- and eight-year-old girls.

They are valuable, and they are certainly worth fighting for. Every day I remind my girls that God's hand is on their lives and how God is using them, and will continue to use them, mightily for His kingdom.

I remember an incident when my youngest, Erica, was very sick with an infection in her chest cavity. We were believing God for her healing. Her dad, her older sister, Kaylee, and I were on the bed, and we were just quietly praying for Erica. All of a sudden, Kaylee rose up on the bed and boldly proclaimed, "Listen, guys, we have to get off this bed, get the anointing oil, and pray for Erica *real hard*." So we sensed that God was really speaking through this little prophet.

We grabbed the anointing oil just in time before Erica got "baptized" with it.

We put some on Kaylee's hands, and she started praying at the top of her lungs, "Father, in the name of Jesus, we rebuke this sickness in Erica. Devil, you are a liar....She is healed by the blood of Jesus. Thank You, Jesus, for her healing."

We all continued to praise God. The very next day Erica woke up completely clear, and God worked a miracle through her big sister. *There is a cause!*

Make your mind up that the devil is not going to have your children whether they are five or fifty.

I am determined that, if Jesus tarries, I will leave a legacy to my children and my grandchildren to start them on their God-given purpose and destiny. And by the grace of God, they will finish it.

I declare to you today that there is a cause for your violent faith. The cause is for your children, your body, your calling, your destiny, your God-given purpose. For the sake of your seed, exercise violent faith and reclaim the territory that the devil has gained some ground on.

Our children are worth it! They are called, chosen, set apart, and the generation that God is raising up to do mighty things. Even at this writing, my eight-year-old has an incredible anointing upon her life. She lays hands on people, and they are healed. She prophesies without any foreknowledge of the person's life, and the prophecy comes to pass. There is nothing or nobody that can come near my two babies because my husband and I have sealed their lives with the blood of Jesus, and they belong to God. The devil cannot have them because they are marked for God, and so are yours.

A Cause to Rejoice

Solomon said there is a right time for everything, "*a time to weep, and a time to laugh*" (Eccles. 3:4, emphasis added). Although in the natural, the situation may be cause for you to weep, in the supernatural it is cause for you to rejoice.

The Bible admonishes us in Jeremiah 31:16, "Refrain thy voice from weeping." God is speaking through Jeremiah announcing the good news of hope. It never pays to let yourself get into a little "pity party" or a "woe-is-me" attitude. Maybe God is telling you to stop crying and get some praise on your lips. His Word says that He has turned "*my mourning into dancing*" (Ps. 30:11, emphasis added). Stop mourning for what you lost, pick yourself up by the bootstraps, and get moving! He also says in His Word, "Remember ye not the former things, neither consider the things of old. Behold, I will do a new thing; now it shall spring forth; shall ye not know it? I will even make a way in the wilderness, and rivers in the desert" (Isa. 43:18–19).

When the children of Israel were caught in what looked like a hopeless situation, God gave Moses a strange command: He told him to quit praying.

Faced with the Red Sea in front of them and the dreadful Egyptian army behind them, it looked like everything was closing in on them. So they do what most people do when confronted with impossibilities: whine.

> And they turned against Moses, *whining*, "Have you brought us out here to die in the desert because there were not enough graves for us in Egypt? Why did you make us leave Egypt? Isn't this what we told you, while we were slaves, to leave us alone? We said it would be better to be slaves to the Egyptians than dead in the wilderness."
> —EXODUS 14:11–12, TLB, EMPHASIS ADDED

Moses, however, encourages them and tries to reassure them that God was going to take care of them.

> But Moses told the people, "Don't be afraid. Just stand where you are and watch, and you will see the wonderful way the Lord will rescue you today. The Egyptians you are looking at—you will never see them again. The Lord will fight for you, and you won't need to lift a finger!" Then the Lord said to Moses, "*Quit praying* and get the people moving! Forward, march!"
> —EXODUS 14:13–15, TLB, EMPHASIS ADDED

Quit praying? Yes, my friend, you read that correctly. There is going to come a point in this walk of violent faith when you will hear the Lord say, "Quit trying to find one more thing to do. Go and do what I've already told you to do."

The problem with us is *not* that we don't have clear instructions; the problem is that we keep bumping into that area of life called *obedience*, which we choose to ignore.

Don't misunderstand me; I'm not saying that God is telling *you* to quit praying permanently. But some of us are looking for new revelations every day, something that will tickle our ears, because, like the children of Israel, we depend on that what we can see and touch—a prophet, the latest book, or the most current tape series. We expect people—not God—to speak to us. (See Exodus 20:19.) The truth of the matter is that unless we get the revelation of this word, we *will* die, along with our dreams, hopes, aspirations, and destinies.

Instead of waiting for a prophetic word or getting a book or cassette that tells us what *we want to hear*, let's rejoice in the fact that our cause is developing in us violent faith. Our present situation—no matter how hopeless it may seem—does not dictate our future. We have a sure word from the Lord that He will see us through our present circumstance, and we have His assurance that prayer works.

Just be aware that on your journey from point A to point Z, a spirit of prevention may try to hinder your cause.

Then he said to me, "Do not fear, Daniel, for from the first day that you set your heart to understand, and to humble yourself before your God, your words were heard; and I have come because of your words. But the prince of the kingdom of Persia withstood me twenty-one days; and behold, Michael, one of the chief princes, came to help me, for I had been left alone there with the kings of Persia."

—DANIEL 10:12–13, NKJV

Chapter Seven

THE SPIRIT OF PREVENTION

M Y HUSBAND AND I were praying about a certain need in our lives and in the ministry, and we had already received a word that the provision was on the way through Him and also through friends of our ministry. The problem was that nothing was happening with our prayers, so we began to set aside some time for fasting, too.

During our time of seeking the Lord, we were awakened one morning at around 3:00 a.m., and God gave us this word: "There is a 'spirit of prevention' that is hindering your prayers from being answered." He took us to the passage of Scripture in the Book of Daniel when Daniel also experienced hindrance from answered prayers. God revealed to us that a "spirit of prevention" is a specific stronghold assigned by the devil to interfere—or prevent—those things that God has promised to us from coming to pass.

God showed us that in order for this spirit to be defeated in our lives, we had to name the stronghold and expose that spirit in order for the breakthrough to come. When we did that, we received our breakthrough.

SPIRIT OF PREVENTION DEFINED

The "spirit of prevention" is that which the enemy uses to disrupt and overturn God's promise of supernatural breakthrough or miracle. It is anything that prevents you from being happy, being prosperous, having health, getting job promotions, having a happy marriage, or coming into your inheritance as a child of God.

For example, if your boss comes up to you and says, "You know,

I have really been watching you. I've seen how hard you work and the excellence with which you work, and I'm going to give you a raise." Then you get excited and tell your family and friends, and you begin to anticipate this raise. Two weeks go by, then two months, and he has not mentioned anything to you since that day. You're left wondering why you haven't gotten the raise. In some instances, he may have forgotten, but more than likely, it is the "spirit of prevention" keeping from you what is rightfully yours and the things that have been promised to you.

If you know what stronghold to fight against, then you can expose it and destroy it in the spirit realm. Then it has to go back to hell from where it came, and, therefore, it is immediately defeated.

If you know that your son or daughter is involved in a homosexual lifestyle, you don't embrace the lifestyle as if to say, "It's OK. I'll love you no matter what decisions you make for your life." No! You expose that spirit for what it is. Whether it is a spirit of promiscuity, unnatural desires, or a spirit of death and destruction, come against it with the blood of Jesus, in the name of Jesus, and with the Word of God; then attack it every day through prayer and fasting.

God revealed to us that this spirit is also known as a "spirit of obstruction." In the courtroom we understand the term "obstruction of justice" to mean that someone has tampered with evidence, held back information, or interfered with an investigation or police work. In the same sense, the devil, who is the author of the spirit of prevention, is keeping you from getting what is rightfully yours. God has already said that it is yours; therefore, it is yours.

Satan's plan is to stop the will of God and the promises of God from being fulfilled in our lives. He will use every means possible to hinder that plan and prevent it from coming to pass.

Such is the case with Daniel, who had almost given up hope after fasting and praying for twenty-one days. The good news is that Satan cannot stop the plan of God, because as you will see with Daniel, delay was not denial.

SPIRITUAL ASSIGNMENTS IN THE HEAVENLIES

In Daniel 10, the Bible says that Daniel prayed and fasted for twenty-one days. But then the Word lays out very plainly that the angel was fighting against the prince of Persia. Why in the world did it take twenty-one days for the answer to come? The post office is faster than that! The angel of the Lord says, "I was sent the first day that you prayed, but because of the prince of the kingdom of Persia that fought against me for twenty-one days, your prayers were hindered, prevented, and obstructed."

Now was he talking about an earthly prince of Persia of that time?

No! Of course not! I can never be convinced that it was some young, handsome prince on this earth to which the angel was referring. No, he was talking about a demonic prince over the Persian Empire coming against a heavenly being. I'm convinced that there are certain spirits that are assigned to certain regions. Satan assigns certain demons for certain cities, regions, countries, people, families, and neighborhoods.

For instance, when you think of the city of Las Vegas, your mind immediately thinks of gambling. When you consider Iran and Iraq, you think of terrorism. When you think about Central and South America, from where most illegal drugs are smuggled into the United States, you think drugs. The inner cities of New York, Detroit, Miami, and Los Angeles are known for their neighborhoods of gangs.

I will never forget when I flew into Amsterdam, Holland, on my way to minister at Youth With A Mission. As the plane was approaching the city and this mammoth airport, I began to pray over the city. Immediately I felt such a feeling of uneasiness and a heaviness in my spirit that made me feel uncomfortable. Going through customs, the border guard asked me for my passport, looked at it, then pulled me out of the line for no apparent reason. The guard made me sit for what I thought would be a routine check. Well, it turned into more than just a routine check. He spoke very roughly to me and insisted that, maybe, I had forged this passport. I was taken to a back room, along with another guard, and was interrogated. They ripped up my passport right in front of my face and then left me alone in the room for, literally, hours.

The other team members who were with me refused to go on without me, and my hosts on the other side of the gate were baffled, wondering if I had missed my flight, gotten sick, or just bailed out on them. All I could do was pray that God would deliver me from the situation. Now I know that may not seem like much to someone who may be reading this right now, and it probably isn't, considering the fact that many people have been tortured, even killed, all for the sake of the gospel. But for this little Native American from North Carolina, it was a very frightening experience. In the end everything turned out all right, but there were some border guards who got in a heap of trouble. By the time the American embassy was finished with them, some heads were spinning!

But here is my point. Amsterdam is known as a very beautiful city, but it is also known as a city of legalized drugs, legalized prostitution, and distribution of hard-core pornography. After many hours of fasting and prayer, being heavily anointed and equipped with violent faith and determination to spread the gospel, the enemy had assigned the "spirit of prevention" to fight me by sending someone to prevent me from entering the country by literally tearing up my passport.

It was at this point that I could have very easily given into this tactic of the enemy and doubted the call of God to go to this country, just as Daniel doubted that God was going to answer his prayer. The Bible says, "We are not ignorant of his [the devil's] schemes" (2 Cor. 2:11, NAS). Being all the more determined to fulfill God's plan, I got past the checkpoint and got busy doing damage on the kingdom of darkness. That part of my trip proved to be the most fruitful of the entire trip. I saw addicts set free, prostitutes come to Jesus, and the church of Jesus Christ was strengthened greatly. We must be quick to recognize the devil's strongholds so that we can overcome him by exposing his schemes and tricks.

HISTORY MAKERS, HEAVEN'S KEEPERS

No one can deny history because it has already happened. On July 20, 1969, at 10:56 p.m. (EDT), Neil Armstrong, the first man to land on the moon, stated, "That's one small step for man, one giant leap for mankind." No one can deny that we put a man on the moon. No one can deny that Abraham Lincoln was our president. It's in the history books. It is on record.

When prophecy has been spoken over your life, it becomes heaven's history. It cannot be denied. You can't deny prophecy, because it has already happened in the heavens, so therefore, it has to happen in the natural. It's in heaven's history book; it's on the record. When Isaiah prophesied, "Behold, a virgin shall conceive and bear a son, and shall call his name Immanuel," it was immediately recorded in the annals of heaven. And we know that prophecy came to pass because Jesus Christ lives in our hearts as a result of His birth, death, burial, and resurrection. Jesus prophesied in Matthew's Gospel that in the last days, "ye shall hear of wars and rumours of wars: see that ye be not troubled: for all these things must come to pass, but the end is not yet. For nation shall rise against nation, and kingdom against kingdom: and there shall be famines, and pestilences, and earthquakes, in divers places," and many other things that are coming on the face of the earth before His return (Matt. 24:6–7). Some of the biblical prophecies concerning the Lord's return have already come to pass. And we know that, even now, Jesus is standing on the precipice of heaven, waiting for the Father's signal to fulfill this final prophecy. When God speaks a word, it is done.

If you have received a prophecy, then grab hold of the promise that it will surely come to pass and walk in it, because it has already been spoken and recorded in the history of heaven. Jesus is right now interceding on your behalf to the Father, and the Father hears every word that the Son prays. All of heaven and hell heard what has been spoken, as the writer of Hebrews said that you "are compassed about with so great a cloud of witnesses" (Heb. 12:1). So it must come to pass because the enemy cannot deny history, and *heaven is keeping record*.

Another strategy of the enemy is to make you think that your prayers are not being heard, that God doesn't hear and answer prayer. I will cover this more in the next chapter, but for now, let's look at what the angel told Daniel.

> For from the first day...your words were heard.
> —DANIEL 10:12, NAS

In other words, the first day the words were uttered out of your mouth, your words were heard in heaven.

The first day you prayed for your family to be saved, God heard your prayer, because the Word of God declares, "Believe on the Lord Jesus Christ, and you will be saved, you and your household" (Acts 16:31, NKJV).

The first day you prayed to be healed, the Word says, "He sent his word, and healed [you]" (Ps. 107:20).

It doesn't matter how you feel or what it may look like. Have faith. God heard your prayers.

A DIVIDED KINGDOM WILL NOT STAND

The next thing the angel told Daniel is, "I called out for Michael (Michael has always been recognized as a warring angel), and Michael came and helped me, and he broke through to deliver your answer. Here is the answer to your prayer. Now I have to go and hurry back to help Michael wrap this thing up." (See Daniel 10:13.) Praise God!

Now what that tells me is that angels strengthen and help each other. If angels help and strengthen each other, is it not also conceivable that demons, which are fallen angels, also help and strengthen each other? Matthew 12:43–45 says:

> When the unclean spirit is gone out of a man, he walketh through dry places, seeking rest, and findeth none. Then he saith, I will

return unto my house from whence I came out; and when he is come, he findeth it empty, swept, and garnished. Then goeth he and *taketh with himself seven other spirits more wicked than himself,* and they enter in and dwell there, and the last state of that man is worse than the first.

—EMPHASIS ADDED

This is very important. When you are attacking and coming against the gates of hell in your life, that kingdom or domain that the devil has set up against you and your life and family is being threatened to fall. So when this happens, those spirits or demons assigned to your life begin to call for help. But when they do that, they are pulling demonic spirits from other kingdoms that they are working on, so their kingdoms are divided.

Mark 3:24–26 says:

If a kingdom be divided against itself, that kingdom cannot stand. And if a house be divided against itself, that house cannot stand. And if Satan rise up against himself, and be divided, he cannot stand, but hath an end.

Here is the great news: there are not enough demons to go around. Do you know how many demons there are? Only one-third! Lucifer was kicked out of heaven along with one-third of the angels. (See Revelations 12:4.) So why does the church magnify demons and devils? We complain of demons in the sound system and demons in the carpet, but the fact remains that only one-third of the angels were kicked out.

There are two-thirds of the heavenly hosts who are for us, two-thirds who are on our side, going before us, protecting us, and encamping around us. Even greater than the angels, we have the Father, Son, and the Holy Spirit on our side.

There is no Mrs. Devil. Not even one demon has enlarged Satan's kingdom. There are no girlfriends, concubines, no little baby demons and devils running around waiting to grow up, and no maternity ward in hell, just one-third. Satan is limited in his strategy to destroy you. He is not the big, bad dude he wants us to think that he is. The Bible says that one day we will look upon him and say, "Can this be the one who shook the earth and kingdoms of the world?" (Isa. 14:16, TLB).

There are three things that you need to know about the devil.

1. He is not omnipotent (all-powerful).

If he really is the all-powerful being that he supposes to be, he would have killed you before you got saved. But the fact of the matter is, there was no demon or devil in hell that could stop you from getting saved.

2. He is not omniscient (all-knowing).

The devil does not know the future; he only knows the present like us. But one thing that he does know about his future is that he will spend an eternity in torment. He does know that, and he trembles.

3. He is not omnipresent (everywhere at once).

Satan can't be here and there at the same time. If he is here, he can't be there, because he is here and not there. How do we know that? Because he is here. Get it!

But Jehovah God is omnipresent. He is everywhere. He is here in Tennessee while I am writing this book. He is in believers' homes in Russia. He is in California. He is in China. He is in the mud huts of Africa. He is everywhere.

When the devil's kingdom is threatened and we are operating in violent faith and attacking his kingdom with prayer, fasting, and standing on the Word, he says, "I need more devils. I have to get some help. I need some reinforcements. What can I do? I know! I'll pull them from other kingdoms!" So he begins to look around and call them from other kingdoms.

But if the church is doing its job in violently attacking with prayer and fasting wherever that kingdom has been divided, that kingdom is going to fall. So whenever he pulls them from other kingdoms, his kingdom will fall and collapse.

The year was 1989. Most of us missed it. The church had been pounding away at the gates of hell over the 1.2 billion people in Communist China. As we all know, the church in China is alive and thriving, and growing by the thousands every day. I don't know about you, but I have prayed for China all of my life. I can remember my mama praying for this country and its people for as long as I have known the Lord. In 1989 the gates of hell over the kingdom of China began to sway, quiver, and shake.

The whole world watched on CNN and all of the other networks as the students in Tiananmen Square rose up and began to march and demonstrate for freedom. We watched tens of thousands of Chinese people experience, for a brief moment, a little taste of freedom and liberty. For just a split second, the devil became afraid, because the gates over China were beginning to shake.

The devil said, "I need them. I need more demons." So he began to look through the earth. "I know what I'll do. I'll pull more devils off the kingdoms of Russia, Bulgaria, Ukraine, Albania, the Czech Republic, East Germany, and Hungary." So when the devil pulled those demons from these countries, he told them, "Leave your kingdom there, and come over to China and help reinforce the kingdom that is over China, because things are very shaky." But when the devil divided his kingdom over Russia and those other republics, overnight Communism fell…atheism fell…agnosticism fell, and Jesus was exalted and lifted high upon the earth. We saw with our very eyes the prophecy come to pass that had been spoken many years ago about a man by the name of Mikhail who would come to power. He would have a mark on his face that would be very prominent and would be the one that would bring freedom and tear the wall down so that the gospel of Jesus Christ could be heard once again. The wall fell, and the gospel of Jesus Christ has been spread all over Eastern Europe in an unprecedented fashion. But we also saw the sobering Word of the Lord come to pass in Mark 3:26.

And if Satan rise up against himself, and be divided, he cannot stand, but hath an end.

HOW TO DEFEAT THE SPIRIT OF PREVENTION

There are three things you must do to defeat the spirit of prevention.

1. Expose it.

You must first of all expose that spirit and name it for who and what it is. If you know its name, then you can address it, and it has no more secrecy or power over you.

The Bible says that:

> A demon-possessed man ran out from a graveyard, just as Jesus was climbing from the boat. This man lived among the grave-stones and had such strength that whenever he was put into handcuffs and shackles—as he often was—he snapped the hand-cuffs from his wrists and smashed the shackles and walked away. No one was strong enough to control him. All day long and through the night he would wander among the tombs and in the wild hills, screaming and cutting himself with sharp pieces of stone.
>
> —MARK 5:2–5, TLB

The Bible says that when Jesus was still far out on the water, the man saw Him and started to run toward Him. When Jesus came on land, the man fell down at His feet. He knew that his deliverance was very near. So the Word says that Jesus commanded the demons, "Come out!"

Then Jesus asked, "What is your name?" And the demon replied, "Legion, for there are many of us here within this man." The first thing Jesus did was to expose them for who they were. One of the main principles to getting deliverance to come in your situation is to expose Satan for who he is. Homosexuality is not an alternative lifestyle. It is not who you were created to be. It is an abomination and a disgrace in the sight of God. Expose it. Call it out. Call it what it is—sin!

If you go into a classroom and tell the kids, "Come here," all of them will come. But if you say, "Susie, come here," or "Johnny, with the blue shirt on, come here," then you have singled out whom you are calling. You have identified that person. The same is true in the spirit realm. We must identify and expose the enemy for who and what he is and what he is doing in our family and lives. Then we will see deliverance come.

2. Identify who you are in Christ.

The next thing in defeating this "spirit of prevention" is to know who you are in Christ, as I covered in chapter four. We must declare and use the Word of God, proclaim the name of Jesus, and apply the blood to this situation.

Recruit people of like faith, like spirit, like anointing, and like destiny to agree with you in prayer for your breakthrough.

3. Overcome the flesh.

The last thing in defeating the spirit of prevention is overcoming your flesh, because one of the major enemies that we fight is our flesh. Paul said that when he wanted to do good, evil was present. The thing that he wanted to do, he didn't do, and the thing that he didn't want to do is what he did. Then he asked, "Who can deliver me from this vile body?" (See Romans 7:15–25.) Thank God, Jesus did, He does, and He will. But the point is that we have to constantly deny our flesh, the thing that is easy, convenient, and fun. We are dealing with demons and devils that are assigned to destroy, and they don't give up easily, so neither can we.

When you have a word to come forth to you through the Word of God that has been quickened by your spirit, through a word of prophecy, or through a season of prayer, the Bible says that immediately a preventive word comes forth from hell to put forth barriers and obstacles. The devil comes to steal that word away from you. (See Mark 4:15.) His job is to steal, kill, destroy, and prevent that word from going forth. (See John 10:10.)

If you wake up in the middle of the night and God is calling you to pray, that is no time to confer with flesh and blood. That is certainly not a good time to be asking yourself, "Now is this God, or is this the devil trying to rob me of my sleep?" You have to get yourself out of the way. Crucify the flesh, and say yes to Jesus.

I know if I wake up in the middle of the night or in the wee hours of the morning, it's God, not me. I might as well get up, pray, and do some warfare, especially if I'm right in the middle of a hellish situation. If I wake up alert as if it were the middle of the afternoon, that is not the time to start counting sheep. God is telling me to get up, intercede, and get the mind of the Spirit.

THE HORSES ARE COMING

I want to leave you with a very powerful vision that I experienced one Sunday morning. All during the service that morning there was an awesome presence of God that was especially rich and real. My husband and I had been fasting during that week and believing God for some mighty things in the ministry. While standing on the church stage, I was ministering in song: "These Are the Days of Elijah," "No God Like Jehovah." There was such a powerful anointing in the room, one that I hadn't experienced with this song ever before. As the song finished and the track stopped, the people continued to worship. It was a very powerful atmosphere. I felt that if I had looked hard enough, I would have been able to see Jesus. His presence felt almost tangible.

As the music stopped, there was no one on the drums; there was no one playing anything with any rhythm, just someone on the organ playing very softly. But inside of me, the rhythm of that song kept going. It was almost like something inside of me was moving with the rhythm, but it had nothing to do with the rhythm. It had to do with what the Spirit of the Lord was trying to tell me. Then I heard a sound.

I said to the Lord, "Lord, what is that?" I asked the pastor, "Do you hear that?"

"No," he said.

But I heard it. It was the sound of horses running. My spirit got a hold of it, and I began to share with the congregation what I was feeling and sensing and hearing. In my spirit I could hear the sound of an entire herd of horses galloping. Then I could see them, and in the spirit, I began to hear their neighing and their sounds of huffing. As we began to worship and get further and deeper into worship, the hoofs began to get louder and louder. I said to the Lord, "Lord, what is that?"

He said to me, "The horses are coming! The horses are coming!"

Then I noticed that everyone was caught up like a cattle round-up in the rhythm of the music being played. But in the spirit God began to show me the horses that were coming.

These were not ordinary horses. They were huge, mammoth, beautiful, white, perfect, stallions. Their manes were long and white, flowing in the wind, and their eyes were ablaze with fire and set with a determination. But that wasn't all. On top of these horses were some of the biggest, most gigantic angels that I have ever seen in my life. I've seen pictures of angels, and I've seen people act as angels in church plays. I have even seen Hollywood try to portray angels, but these beings were unlike anything I have ever seen or recognized. Their bodies were curved and shaped perfectly as if they worked out every day in a gym. Their muscles protruded, and even their faces were as perfect as anything I could ever imagine. Their faces were the faces from different ethnic backgrounds, which let me know that all of us were represented in the heavenly hosts before the world was ever created. Their silky hair was flowing in the air.

That wasn't the end of this vision, because not only were there horses and angels, but also on the backs of these angels were backpacks. But they were not your ordinary backpacks. These backpacks were as big as suitcases.

God spoke to me and said, "Inside of those bags are the promises that I have given to you through My Word. Each horse represents what you have been believing for. There are horses of finances, horses of healing for your family, horses of anointing, horses of boldness, authority, faith, grace, peace, restoration. The horses are coming! The horses are coming!"

As I looked, the horses kept getting closer and closer. He reminded me of the scripture from Daniel 10, and He said, "They are almost here, because Michael has broken through. Michael has broken through. The prince of the kingdom of Persia has withstood him, but he has broken through."

As I heard the Lord saying this, I shared it with the church, and the worship just kept getting higher and higher.

Then the last thing that I saw in the vision was the whole herd galloping through the heavens. And the one at the very head of the herd was "one like unto the Son of man, clothed with a garment down to the foot, and girt about the paps with a golden girdle. His head and his hairs were white like wool, as white as snow; and his eyes were as a flame of fire; and his feet like unto fine brass, as if they burned in a furnace; and his voice as the sound of many waters. And he had in his right hand seven stars; and out of his mouth went a sharp twoedged sword; and his countenance was as the sun shineth in his strength" (Rev. 1:13–16).

I'm telling you, I have never seen or heard anything like that in my entire life. I can assure you that the very next week, breakthrough after breakthrough began to happen in our lives. Financial breakthroughs, healings, deliverances, and miracles came. I am still believing for mighty things to come to pass.

I can tell you and encourage you, on the authority of God's Word, your answer is on the way. The horses are coming! Don't quit praying. Like Daniel, be determined to persevere. Worship God because the angels are fighting on your behalf. Don't praise Him *when* the answer comes. Praise Him *until* the answer comes, and, by all means, don't quit. Prayer works!

Call unto me, and I will answer thee, and shew thee great and mighty things, which thou knowest not.

—JEREMIAH 33:3

Therefore I say unto you, what things soever ye desire, when ye pray, believe that ye receive them, and ye shall have them.

—MARK 11:24

The prayer of a righteous man has great power in its effects.

—JAMES 5:16, RSV

Zion, deep in your heart you cried out to the Lord. Now let your tears overflow your walls day and night. *Don't ever lose hope* or let your tears stop. Get up and pray for help all through the night. Pour out your feelings to the Lord, as you would pour water out of a jug. Beg him to save your people.

—LAMENTATIONS 2:18–19, CEV, EMPHASIS ADDED

Chapter Eight

DON'T QUIT, PRAYER WORKS

O N OCTOBER 29, 1941, United Kingdom Prime Minister Winston Churchill visited Harrow School to hear the traditional songs he had sung there as a youth, as well as to speak to the students. This became one of his most quoted speeches. Churchill stood before the students and said:

> Never give in. Never, never, never, never, never, in nothing great or small, large or petty, never give in except to convictions of honor and good sense. Never give in to force; never yield to the apparently overwhelming might of the enemy.[1]

There was someone greater than a Churchill who came thousands of years earlier that told us something very similar, but His words were not from human origin. He was the Son of God, and under the inspiration of the Holy Spirit, the writer of Hebrews admonishes us:

> Do not throw away this confident trust in the Lord, *no matter what happens.* Remember the great reward it brings you! *Patient endurance is what you need now,* so you will continue to do God's will. Then you will receive all that He has promised.
> —HEBREWS 10:35, NLT, EMPHASIS ADDED

There is one prayer that I have prayed often for you while writing this book, and that is that you would not lose heart and abort the plan of God for your life. "Patient endurance" is what the Bible says we need in order to do the will of God concerning what we are believing for.

The word *endurance* can take on many meanings: "stamina," "determination," "vigor," "grit," "strength," "fortitude."

All of these words combined together, I believe, can be summed up with the subject of this book. Faith, endurance, and determination are what the men and women of God used to see prayer answered in some remarkable ways under some astonishing circumstances.

THE INFLUENCE AND POWER OF PRAYER

In the introduction, the first paragraph reads, "There is nothing more effective on the face of this earth than the power of prayer and the far-reaching hand of faith. Prayer and faith fit together like a beautiful symphony of orchestral music. Never underestimate them, for they have *altered the course of nature, changed the laws of the universe, and have even influenced and changed the mind of God.*"

Let's look at the first one: "altered the course of nature."

Nature, as we know it, is made up of many things around us: the earth, the heavens, the sea, sun, stars, mountains, trees, grass, flowers, birds, and everything that is beautiful. David said:

> When I consider thy heavens, the work of thy fingers, the moon and the stars, which thou hast ordained; what is man, that thou art mindful of him? and the son of man, that thou visitest him?
> —PSALM 8:3–4

> Day and night alike belong to you; you made the starlight and the sun. All nature is within your hands; you make the summer and the winter too.
> —PSALM 74:16–17, TLB

The natural world is everything that the Father has made for our good pleasure, but nothing is more important on the face of this planet than His children. There is a Bible story that proves He will move heaven and earth if He has to, and respond to the cries of His people. It is a story of hope. It is a story of deliverance and the unfathomable love that Father God has for us and the amazing things He will do to answer prayer.

The children of Israel left Egypt fleeing Pharaoh's fury because of all the horrible plagues and set out for the Promised Land. But Pharaoh, having realized the great loss that had occurred in his country, decided to go after the fleeing Israelites. As they trekked through the wilderness, the Egyptian army with chariots and horses advanced. With the Red Sea in front of them, the Egyptian army behind them, and mountains surrounding them, the children of Israel were in a very bad predicament.

When you step out and begin to walk in obedience, expect opposition. God never told you that you were going to float through life on this violent faith path and never have another problem. But He did promise, "When thou passest through the waters, I will be with thee; and through the rivers, they shall not overflow thee" (Isa. 43:2).

Facing all of this opposition, the Israelites "were sore afraid: and the children of Israel cried out unto the Lord." Now here is where it really begins to get interesting. God was about to alter the very laws of nature that He created. The children of Israel were about to get a surprise that they would never experience again and see the miracle-working power of God in an awesome way.

The people began to whine and cry out to the Lord and Moses, and they chided Moses for even bringing them to this point. When panic strikes your life, remember God always has a plan. Just stop, take a deep breath, and listen for the voice of the Lord. You will hear it distinctly say, "This is the way, walk ye in it" (Isa. 30:21).

Moses, however, began to encourage the people, and God told him exactly what to do. Under the command of the Lord, Moses lifted up his rod and stretched it out over the Red Sea:

> *And the LORD caused the sea to go back* by a strong east wind all that night, *and made the sea into dry land,* and the waters were divided. So the children of Israel went into the midst of the sea

119

on the *dry ground:* and the waters were a wall to them on their right hand and on their left.

—EXODUS 14:21–22, NKJV, EMPHASIS ADDED

Wow! How incredible was that? Can you imagine the kids going through that divided sea looking up at that water, watching schools of fish swimming and whales and dolphins playing? This was undoubtedly the very first aquarium, but without the glass. I bet they were saying, "Cool!" OK, maybe not. But it really was cool!

You can't even begin to imagine all of the prayers that God is going to answer for you too if you'll just keep believing and don't quit praying. You may be faced with troubled waters all around you, but you serve a God who is the same yesterday, today, and forever. If He can alter the very course of nature to move on behalf of His children at the Red Sea, then surely He can speak to *your* Red Sea and divide the waters in your life today. He will move heaven and earth and stop the sun and the moon in their tracks if it means answering your prayers.

INTERRUPTED LAWS OF THE UNIVERSE

Not only can God alter the course of nature, but He can also interrupt the laws of the universe. After all, He instituted them!

The Bible states in Proverbs 18:21, "Death and life are in the power of the tongue." That means your mouth has the ability to speak and receive everything for which you believe God to do. You also have the potential to speak death and destruction to your circumstances. James makes it very clear how much damage the words we speak can inflict upon our lives.

The tongue is a small thing, but what enormous damage it can do.... The tongue is a flame of fire. It is full of wickedness, and poisons every part of the body.... The tongue is set on fire by hell itself and can turn our whole lives into a blazing flame of destruction and disaster.

—JAMES 3:5–6, TLB

The good news is the victory that you are waiting for is also in your mouth. The Bible states, "The word [of faith] is nigh thee, even in thy mouth" (Rom. 10:8). Paul said, "Be careful for nothing; but in every thing by prayer and supplication *with thanksgiving* let your requests be made known unto God" (Phil. 4:6, emphasis added). I believe that when we speak the Word of God and combine that with praise and thanksgiving, we are speaking life. On the other hand, when we talk the talk of defeat or talk negatively of our circumstances, we are allowing death to be spoken over our lives.

One thing that I don't want to do is to confuse this teaching with something that seems far-fetched—some pie-in-the-sky—"if you name it and claim it, then you'll get it." That is not my stance. However, I do believe in "[calling] things that are not as though they were" (Rom. 4:17, NIV). I do believe in saying what the Word says that I am, and I believe in having and going after what the Word says that I can have. I also believe in being realistic. I know the facts can be overwhelming, but I also understand what the truth of the Word is. I don't know about you, but I would much rather have truth over facts. Jesus said, "If ye abide in me, and my words abide in you, ye shall ask what ye will, and it shall be done unto you" (John 15:7).

THE PRAYER OF JUST ONE

After the Flood, God made a covenant with Noah that He would not disrupt His plan for mankind, and He gave mankind the assurance that as long as the earth remains, things will continue the way that He intended for them to be from the beginning.

> While the earth remaineth, seedtime and harvest, and cold and heat, and summer and winter, and day and night shall not cease.
>
> —GENESIS 8:22

But in the Book of Joshua we find where God interrupted even the very law of His universe. This is another phenomenal story of how the Father will go to any length to help His children and answer their prayers.

The Bible says, "The five kings of the Amorites... gathered themselves together, and went up... and made war against [Joshua and the children of Israel]" (Josh. 10:5).

As the sun set on the battle, Joshua was determined to finish what he started because he had a word from God. God told him not to fear, because He was going to give his enemies into their hands:

> Joshua prayed aloud, "Let the sun stand still over Gibeon, and let the moon stand still in its place, over the valley of Aijalon!" And the sun and the moon didn't move until the Israeli army had finished the destruction of its enemies!... So the sun stopped there in the heavens and stayed there for almost twenty-four hours! There had never been such a day before, and there has never been another day since, when the Lord stopped the sun and the moon—*all because of the prayer of one man.*
> —JOSHUA 10:12–14, TLB, EMPHASIS ADDED

How awesome is that, that God would actually break one of the laws of the universe? The sun setting and the moon rising are as natural as the seasons, as natural as the ocean waters coming so far and then receding, as natural as a human being breathing the breath that God sends through the lungs. But God can do anything He wants because of the simple fact that He is God. He holds the cup in His hand, and He turns it whichever way He wishes. (See Psalm 75:8.) I love it when He says with such audaciousness, "I am God... and there is no other like me" (Isa. 46:9, TLB).

WHEN YOU PRAY

The Bible says this happened "all because of the prayer of one man." I believe in the old saying, "Praying people get prayers answered."

Jesus said, "*When* you pray," not *if*, or just in case an opportunity would present itself, but very emphatically, "*when* you pray," as if to say, "This is to be done without even thinking about it." There seems to be an epidemic of prayerlessness that has hit the church in recent years that is numbing.

God told the children of Israel in Numbers 15:1–2, "The Lord told Moses to give these instructions to the people of Israel, '*When* your children finally live in the land I am going to give them…'" (TLB). Not *if*, but *when*. The children of Israel couldn't see the promises of God. They couldn't see themselves in the Promised Land flowing with milk and honey. All they could see were the giants, enemies on every hand, the cloud by day, the fire by night, and all that manna. But God had emphatically given them a time frame—a "when." In other words, "I know what it looks like and what it might seem like, but I have spoken and I cannot go back on My Word." God is bound by His Word, which is the reason why we must remind God of what He said.

If God said "when" back then, He is still saying "when" today. Everything that God has said shall—and will—come to pass.

Paul said, "Being confident [fully persuaded] of this very thing, that he which hath begun a good work in you will perform [finish] it until the day of Jesus Christ" (Phil 1:6). You pay your tithe because you are fully persuaded that "God shall supply all your need according to His riches in glory by Christ Jesus" (Phil 4:19, NKJV). Fully persuaded, fully convinced that God *is going to do* what God said in His Word that He will do. Fully persuaded that you will possess the land that God said is yours.

God told the children of Israel to go in and possess the land. But when they got there to possess it, there were giants occupying it. Now may I tell you something? There will always be giants to oppose you and intimidate you. But God has given you purpose, destiny, and abundant grace to finish what He started in your life. Through prayer and violent faith you can stand firm in your confession and believe who God says you are.

My dear friend Dr. Myles Munroe states in his book *Understanding the Purpose and Power of Prayer*, "Prayer is man giving God the legal right and permission to interfere in earth's affairs."[2] Yielded and effective prayer is saying to God, "I give you permission to do what you want to do in my life, when you want to do it, how you want to do it, and where you want to do it." One thing is for sure; prayer is not an option to the believer. Jesus said, "When you pray," and in another passage He said, "When you fast," meaning such things are expected.

Jesus said, "Men ought always to pray and not to faint or give up." In another passage, He says to "pray without ceasing" (1 Thess. 5:17). This would suggest a continual conversation, a practice that is not unique or something special to be done at certain times or seasons. Jesus plainly instructed us, *don't quit praying.* "The earnest prayer of a righteous man has great power and wonderful results" (James 5:16, TLB). The key to effective prayer is found in Mark 9:23, "If thou canst believe, all things are possible to him that believeth."

God can shut the mouths of the lions, deliver from a fiery furnace, open up the Red Sea, or command the sun and moon to stand still, simply because that's what needs to be done for one of His children.

God doesn't want all of us to quit our jobs, abandon daily life as we know it, and join a monastery to spend the rest of our lives in continuous prayer. But what He does want and expect from us is to stay in communication with Him throughout our day—*on purpose*—speaking praises, prayers, and petitions and filling our minds with thoughts of Him. Speak things such as, "I love You," "You are my God," "You are the great God," "You are working everything out for my good," "You are with me, so I will not fear," or anything else that comes to mind that you want to say to Him. The Word promises, "Thou wilt keep him in perfect peace, whose mind is stayed on thee: because he trusteth in thee" (Isa. 26:3).

TESTIMONY OF EFFECTIVE PRAYER

I was in a church preaching this message on violent faith, and in the congregation was a couple who had not heard from their eighteen-year-old son in six months. You can imagine the anxiety and stress that was on their life, but amid all of the discouragement there was a hope that could not be shaken. They had an enduring faith that their boy was alive and, yes, they were going to hear from him any day, although it had been months since the last time they had heard from him.

As I began to share this very powerful message, hope leaped inside their hearts as never before. They told me that their son was a drug dealer, a drug abuser, an alcoholic, a gang member, and was constantly in trouble with the police. We began to pray at approximately 8:30 that night. As we were praying, simultaneously, this kid was downtown in this huge metropolitan city with a gun in his hand about to hold up a liquor store. All of a sudden, the power of God came upon him, and he started to shake violently.

Two other guys who were with him saw this sudden change that came over their partner in crime and asked, "What's the matter with you? Why are you doing that? Stop shaking!"

The young man told them, "I'm sorry, man, I can't quit shaking. Something is happening to me right now! Here, take my gun. I have to get out of here."

The other guys warned him, "No, man. You're not leaving us here by ourselves. We planned to do this thing together, so let's do it!"

By this time, the kid was very alarmed and didn't quite understand what was happening to his body, so he just took off running.

He ran past many city blocks trying to shake off this shaking. A Spirit-filled police officer saw him running and took off after him. (Isn't it good to know that God will always have strategic people at strategic places to establish His will in our lives?)

The police officer finally caught up with him, with no foreknowledge of what happened to him a few blocks away, and said to him, "Hey, buddy, where are you going so fast?"

The kid responded to the police officer as he stood there still shaking and said, "Sir, I'm trying to get home to my mom and dad. Something is happening to me right now."

The police officer said, "Son, do you have a call of God on your life?"

The boy responded, "Yes sir. Ever since I was twelve years old God called me to preach, and I've been running ever since."

The police officer told him, "Come on, let's get in my squad car. I'll take you home. You have to get your life straightened out with God, son."

Meanwhile, the mom and dad had just returned from church, and they were shouting. "Praise God! Thank You, Jesus! I don't know how it's going to happen, but I know You're going to bring our boy home. Hallelujah!"

Suddenly, there was a knock at the door. The dad opened the door, and standing there was the police officer with the dad's missing son. The dad grabbed his son, embraced him, and joyfully called to his wife.

"Son, where have you been? We've been so worried about you!"

Still shaking under the power of God, the son replied, "Dad, what were you and Mom doing around 8:30 tonight?"

"Son, your mom and I were praying, taking you back from the hand of the enemy and commanding you to come home."

He said, "I knew it! Around 8:30 tonight, something came all over me, and I started shaking and haven't been able to quit yet. Will you please pray for me? I want Jesus in my life."

Right there they led their son in the sinner's prayer, and God set him free. God answered the parents' prayer.

The principle here is you can't give up praying. God answers prayer the way He wants to, how He wants to, and when He wants to. Our job is to ask in faith, believe, and then praise Him until we see our prayer answered. Someone once said, "He may not come when you want Him to, but He is always right on time."

"Now faith is the substance [something solid] of things hoped for, the evidence [convincing proof] of things not seen" (Heb.11:1). Anybody can praise God when his children are saved, his body is healed, and his finances are flourishing, but how about when the opposite is true? That's when you know Him to be your El Shaddai, the all-sufficient One. He supplies all your needs. He is the healer. He is looking out for you simply because His Word says so.

WHAT DOES "PRAY THROUGH" MEAN?

I don't think that we, the church, understand the price that previous generations paid concerning prayer. When my mother would shut herself up in her prayer closet, I didn't know when I would see her again. My mom believed in praying until she prayed through. "Praying through" is not a popular term these days or even a term with which people are familiar.

What does it mean to "pray through"? Jesus told His disciples to stay in the upper room *until* they were endowed with power from on high. Jacob told the angel, "I will not let you go until you bless me."

"Praying through" is tarrying in prayer *until* you know that the burden has been lifted. It is staying there in intercession *until* you feel a release in your spirit. It is praying *until* the peace comes and you know that everything is going to be all right. There is nothing to prove it, except the Word of God, so you stand on what the Word says and praise God until you see the manifestation of your prayer answered.

The Word of God boldly states, "If my people, which are called by name, shall humble themselves, and pray, and seek my face, and turn from their wicked ways; then will I hear from heaven" (2 Chron. 7:14). I believe with all my heart that as much as we want to hear from heaven, God wants to hear from His people on earth. Not because we need anything, although James plainly states, "You have not because you ask not," but more importantly because the God of the universe wants to have an up-close and personal relationship with His children.

My two girls are small right now, but if Jesus tarries, I always want us to have a very close and personal relationship with each other. It's the same way with the Father God. He wants to hear from us every day. He wants communion with us every day just as we would do with a best friend.

Paul wrote:

> Praying always with all prayer and supplication in the Spirit, and watching thereunto with all perseverance and supplication for all saints.
>
> —Ephesians 6:18

Perseverance means to continue to do something in spite of difficulty or opposition; to persist.

To be persistent means to never give up.

Supplication is an entreaty, continual strong and incessant pleadings (never ceasing, repeated endlessly, to be constant) *until the prayer is answered.*

It's like having the kind of faith where you won't turn loose until you receive what you are believing for—a "bulldog" kind of faith. A bulldog is considered one of the toughest, most stubborn types of dogs. That's the kind of faith you should have, the kind that says, "I will not let You go until You bless me."

Paul wrote these powerful words to the church at Ephesus. He was giving us guidelines to follow to show us how to tear down the strongholds of the enemy in our lives and see our prayers answered.

Jesus said concerning perseverance, "Keep on asking, and you will be given what you ask for. Keep on looking, and you will find. Keep on knocking, and the door will be opened" (Matt. 7:7, NLT).

I hear so many people say, "Judy, I just want to give up. What else can I do? I have prayed and nothing has happened. It's too much work. It's too hard. I think I'll turn this burden over to the pastor and let him handle it. What can I do?" Let me tell you what you can do: *don't give up—pray again!* The responsibility is upon us. That is *our* son or daughter, *our* body, *our* home, *our* ministry. Sometimes we have to get up and do *something.*

You may be feeling right now that you have persevered. You have tried, cried, prayed, and fasted, but still no results. With as much compassion as I can write this, I would tell you that God is not moved so much with your tears, although He is "touched with the feeling of our infirmities" (Heb. 4:15), but what moves Him more than anything else is faith—violent faith!

Entering the forces of darkness to take back what's rightfully yours takes courage, unwavering faith, determination, and perseverance. It is not for sissies, the faint of heart, or for people with a slothful spirit. But it is for people who have seen what the devil is doing in their lives and have had it. They would say, "This is it. I am drawing the blood line today. It will never be the same again." They have determined—through prayer, fasting, and coming into agreement with other believers of like faith—that things will change. It means to have the faith of God. Romans 4:17 says, "And this promise is from God himself, who makes the dead live again and speaks of future events with as much certainty as though they were already past" (TLB).

As far as God is concerned, it is already done!

When you become violent in your faith, you will find yourself doing, saying, and acting in ways that will cause everyone around you to stare in wonder asking themselves, *What in the world has happened to him?* Your entire countenance will change.

The devil knows the look of violent faith, and he is afraid of it. A person who has the look of violent faith walks around with a determination and authority on his face that no situation can hinder, because he is walking in faith and he knows *that he knows* God is going to come through for him. That person will begin to see and understand things in the Spirit that are not revealed to everyone. God will cause creativity to emerge from within him, defeating the darkness around him that will leave him astounded.

God will cause your spirit to rise up and give you strategic spiritual-warfare instruction that will bring so much confusion to the enemy's camp he won't know what to do. Things will begin to

129

change and shift on your behalf, and it will amaze you.

The devil wants you to give up on your family. He wants you to feel you have no hope, to accept your situation and say, "That's just the way it is; this is my lot in life," and to give up on those valuable possessions that are precious to you. But we must not forget that the devil is a liar! He cannot tell the truth, because the truth is not in him. When he tells you there is no hope, you must realize the opposite is the truth. You have all hope and promise in Jesus Christ. Praise God!

ALL THINGS ARE POSSIBLE

Jesus said, "With God all things are possible" (Matt. 19:26). *All* means "everything." There are no ifs, ands, or buts about that scripture. The Word means what it says and says what it means. I believe the phrase "with God" is the key to the "all" word. I love what Mark 11:24 says, "Listen to me! You can pray for anything, and if you believe, you have it; it's yours" (TLB). The problem is that too many times we try to accomplish the "all" and leave out the "with God."

Know, and believe, that something is stirring in the heavens. For you even to have this book in your hand and be reading it is a sure sign that God is up to something. I believe in divine appointments and destinies. I know that there have been critical times in my life when I needed a *rhema* word from the Lord. I have seen occasions where God would use an anointed book to speak that word into my spirit.

God is telling me this is your year of recovery. You will get out of debt, you will lose that weight and keep it off, your loved one will be saved, your body will be healed in Jesus' name, you will have the money to buy that house, and you will be able to sell your house and property. Right now God is active in your situation. Keep praying, and don't quit.

Now here is my question. How long are you going to stand there and passively allow the enemy to steal your most valuable possessions? Don't you think it is time to get violent in faith and believe God for the impossible? You won't believe how ready He is to show Himself strong to you. So come on, don't you dare put this book down. Get busy, and don't quit believing. There is some territory to take back, and you are about to "lose your mind" in order to have the mind of Christ.

But God hath chosen the foolish things of the world to confound the wise; and God hath chosen the weak things of the world to confound the things which are mighty. And base things of the world, and things which are despised, hath God chosen, yea, and things which are not, to bring to nought things that are: That no flesh should glory in his presence.

—1 Corinthians 1:27–29

Chapter Nine

CRAZY TURNAROUND FAITH

WHAT IS IT that would cause a prophet, a man of God, to walk around naked for three years without even a pair of sandals on? (See Isaiah 20.) What is it that would cause another man of God to go and "marry a prostitute"? (See Hosea 1:2.) Why would Abraham listen to the voice of God, when God tells him to leave everything that is familiar and comfortable and go to a foreign land not knowing where to go or what to expect? (See Genesis 12.) What would cause the Son of God to spit on the ground and make mud to put on somebody's eyes so that they could see? (See John 9.) Why would Peter and John grab hold of a lame man's hand who had been lame since his birth and command him to walk? (See Acts 3.)

Radical, crazy faith doesn't seem rational in the natural. Nevertheless, this kind of faith moves God, and He honors it.

CRAZY TURNAROUND FAITH DEFINED

One of the things that I have learned is that sometimes you will be stretched beyond your comfort zone, and God will challenge you to go to deeper and higher levels of faith than you could have ever imagined. Oftentimes those levels will seem crazy, fanatical, and extreme, but occasionally, that is what God will require of us because, "As the heavens are higher than the earth, so are my ways higher than your ways, and my thoughts than your thoughts" (Isa. 55:9).

Even at an early age, I have always had a desire to follow hard after the Lord and to go to new levels of maturity in God and, as Paul states, "from glory to glory" (2 Cor. 3:18). That drive to pursue holiness and right standing with God and to possess a radical and violent faith, as I have stated many times, was rooted primarily by godly parents and siblings who, by example, taught me the ways of the Lord. What I have learned, and am still learning, is that I have to be careful in my walk with the Lord. I think that sometimes we are looking for *confirmation*, but what we need is *revelation*. Quite often God will provoke us to move to higher levels that may make us feel uncomfortable.

I know there have been times in my life when I have felt like I have committed the sin of "satisfaction." That is, just being satisfied with my relationship with the Lord and not wanting to go deeper and higher, because one thing that I have learned, "to whom much is given, from him much will be required" (Luke 12:48, NKJV). But the Word doesn't say faith comes by what you have *heard* (past tense), but "faith cometh by *hearing*, and hearing by the word of the God" (Rom. 10:17, emphasis added). There are new and fresh revelations and instructions that the Father wants to give us every day. Jeremiah wrote, "His compassions fail not. They are new every morning: great is thy faithfulness" (Lam. 3:22–23). Paul said, "I press toward the...prize" (Phil. 3:14), and he encouraged us to "stir up the gift" (2 Tim. 1:6) and to "fight the good fight of faith" (1 Tim. 6:12).

The reason we get satisfied is because we get so comfortable in our relationship with the Lord, and we don't want to be uncomfortably stretched in our faith or in our knowledge of the Word, or to be challenged to get out of our comfort zone. The children of Israel told Moses, "Speak thou with us...but let not God speak with us, lest we die" (Exod. 20:19); many of us think the same way. We want to hear a "thus saith the Lord" from someone else, but we don't want to take the time to draw near to Him for ourselves because we are afraid of what He might tell us or of what He might require of us.

I don't know if you have ever been at a point in your life when you did an assessment on your walk with the Lord and thought to yourself, *There has to be more*. Well, that is exactly what happened to my husband and me. Although we were in full-time ministry, we found ourselves asking, "What's next, Lord? We are ready for the next level." Consequently, what did happen next was something that totally revolutionized our spirits and lives and gave new meaning to the definition of "crazy faith."

God began to deal radically with us about prayer and fasting. He called us to a forty-day fast, and we began our pursuit to seek the face of God with a greater passion. As a result of that fast, one day while in prayer, God spoke to me specifically about an all-night prayer vigil. When He first dropped that into my spirit, all I could envision were childhood memories of all-night prayer vigils at my home church.

Every New Year's Eve, a handful of people, mostly composed of elderly saints, would gather around the altar waiting for the new year to arrive. Then finally (after what seemed like days to me), the clock would strike midnight, and we would all breathe a sigh of relief, get into our cars, drive home, and go to bed. I told the Lord, "Father, that is the last thing that I want to be involved in—something with no life and void of Your Spirit and anointing."

But God had more than that in mind for us. These were godly people who had a heart for God, but they were missing the key ingredient: His presence, not tradition. By tradition, I mean "this is how we have always done it, so let's do it and get it over with, so that we can say that we have done it."

The one thing that kept pounding in my spirit over and over again was this phrase that sounded almost like a sing-song: "In order to have something that you have never had before, sometimes you have to do something you have never done before."

I don't remember where I first heard this expression, but it just would not let me rest. God reminded us of so many things that we were believing Him for: salvation of some family members, a breakthrough in ministry opportunities, and also for my husband's brother and his wife, who after nineteen years of marriage still couldn't conceive. There were so many desperate needs and situations in our family that we felt as if there just had to be a change.

Back to Basics

I was somewhat surprised when He took us back to the fundamentals of walking out a Christian life—prayer, fasting, faith, and obedience. The Bible is very clear what the stance of every believer should be: "For therein is the righteousness of God revealed from faith to faith: as it is written, The just shall live by faith" (Rom. 1:17).

Once again He reminded us of what faith is:

> [Faith] is the confident assurance that something we want is going to happen. It is the certainty that what we hope for is waiting for us, even though we cannot see it up ahead.
> —Hebrews 11:1, TLB

Then He went on in verse 6 (TLB) with His little lesson on faith.

> You can never please God without faith, without depending on him. Anyone who wants to come to God must believe that there is a God and that he rewards those who sincerely look for him.

It is not enough to believe that there is a God. The Bible says that even demons believe and tremble (James 2:19). It's more than knowing that there is a God. First, you must believe that He is and that He is a rewarder of those who diligently seek after Him.

Who Is He?

Everything that we need is in Him and in Him alone.

He is *Jehovah Jireh!* He is the God who sees my needs and then provides for those needs (Phil. 4:19).

He is *Jehovah Nissi!* He is the Lord my victory, my standard, and my banner, because "when the enemy comes in like a flood, the Spirit of the Lord will lift up a standard against him" (Isa. 59:19, NKJV). He is the Lord my banner, because "his banner over me [is] love" (Song of Sol. 2:4).

136

He is *Jehovah Shalom,* the God of my peace. "Thou wilt keep him in perfect peace, whose mind is stayed on thee: because he trusteth in thee" (Isa. 26:3).

He is *Jehovah Rapha,* my healer. "He was wounded for our transgressions, he was bruised for our iniquities: the chastisement of our peace was upon him; and with his stripes we are healed" (Isa. 53:5). The Word declares that, "He sent his word, and healed them" (Ps. 107:20).

He is *Jehovah Shammah;* He is always with me. He says, "I will never leave thee, nor forsake thee" (Heb. 13:5).

He is *Jehovah Sabbaoth;* He is my strong deliverer. David said, "I sought the LORD, and he heard me, and delivered me from all my fears" (Ps. 34:4).

He is God, and above Him there is no other, but He is also "a rewarder of those who diligently seek him." Jeremiah declared, "When you come looking for me, you'll find me. Yes, when you get serious about finding me and want it more than anything else…I'll turn things around for you" (Jer. 29:13–14, THE MESSAGE).

We did as God commanded us with these prayer vigils and prayed from ten o'clock at night until six o'clock the next morning. These were some of the most awesome times of praise, worship, fellowship, and communion with the Father that I have ever experienced. We would pray for each other, our nation, our president, his cabinet, the nations of the world, the nation of Israel, prayer requests that would come from literally around the world via e-mails, and requests that came in from pastors. As of this writing, four years later we are still actively involved in these prayer vigils but on a different time frame. We are still seeing the miraculous take place in people's lives.

God kept pounding this prayer, persistence, faith, and obedience thing over and over again: "The just shall live and walk by faith. In order to have something you have never had before, sometimes you have to do something you have never done before." It seemed like a broken record in my mind and in my spirit.

What God impressed upon me was that He desired my commitment to walk in faith and obedience to His will for my life more than anything else. It was not about doing twenty-five ministry opportunities per month, fasting two weeks per month, or going into seclusion eight hours a day. No. He wanted me to be balanced, focused, and sensitive to His Spirit every day through prayer and reading the Word. He challenged me to be willing to do everything that He asked, every time He asked me to do it, in obedience, with excellence, and to do it with power, boldness, and authority.

James outlines so vividly what the Father expects of His children concerning faith and obedience.

> My brethren, pay no servile regard to people [show no prejudice, no partiality]. Do not [attempt to] hold [and] practice the faith of our Lord Jesus Christ [the Lord] of glory [together with snobbery]!...So also faith, if it does not have works (deeds and actions of obedience to back it up), by itself is destitute of power (inoperative and dead). But someone will say [to you then], You (say you) have faith, and I have (good) works. Now you show me your [alleged] faith apart from any (good) works...[if you can], and I by [good] works [of obedience] will show you my faith.... You see a man is justified (pronounced righteous before God) through what he does and not alone through faith [through works of obedience as well as by what he believes]....For as the human body apart from the spirit is lifeless, so faith apart from [its] works of obedience is also dead.
> —JAMES 2:1, 17–18, 24, 26, AMP

Professing your faith isn't enough. You have to put that faith into *action*.

One day while relaxing in the food court of a mall with our family, the girls had gone to get some ice cream with their caregiver, and Jamie and I were just sitting chatting with each other.

Out of nowhere a man walks up to our table and says to my husband, "Excuse me, sir, I don't mean to bother you, but I noticed that you and your family did not finish all the food on your plates. I am homeless, and I haven't eaten in a couple of days. I was wondering if I could have the leftovers."

Well, by this time both of us were just about in tears. My husband says to the man, "Sir, I would not even think of feeding you leftovers. It would be my privilege to buy you anything that you want to eat in this food court with one condition: please allow me the opportunity to tell you about Jesus while you eat." He agreed.

As he sat there gulping down the food, he listened very intently. When he was finished eating, my husband said a prayer with him and sent him on his way.

But what if the scenario had been different? What if my husband would have said, "Well, sir, I tell you what, sit down here and let me tell you about Jesus Christ first. I know you may be hungry, but what you need more than anything is Jesus." That man would not have heard one word my husband would have attempted to say to him if he would have stayed and listened, because first and foremost, he was hungry and needed to eat. Anyone with common sense knows the primary focus in a situation such as that is to meet the basic needs in a person's life and then present him the gospel. It's like telling a drowning man, "First of all, let me tell you about Jesus before I throw you the life preserver."

Faith without works is dead, useless, void, of no effect. That is what James is saying here. "Come on, use some common sense; show me your faith without your works, and I'll show you my faith, with my works." The Bible says, "He that winneth souls is wise" (Prov. 11:30). That doesn't mean that if you win people to Jesus you are smart. It means that if you want to win people to Jesus, you have to use common sense, wisdom, tact, and plain old horse sense. Be careful that you don't embarrass them, but rather win them over with your godly character by being nice to them and using the wisdom that God gives to see their lives changed.

It's Turnaround Time

So as I am pursuing this "in order to have what you have never had before" faith, God takes me on this "crazy faith" journey. Right in the middle of this forty-day fast, I was awakened one morning, very early, and felt such an urge to go into the family room. It was unlike anything I had ever experienced before. Even as I pulled the covers back to slip out of bed, I was so overwhelmed with the presence of God that I fell to the floor, and I literally had to crawl my way into the family room.

As I got into the family room, there was such an overwhelming presence of God that I completely covered myself from head to toe with my prayer shawl. I was afraid to look around and see an angel or some sort of angelic being. I now know, a little, how John and Daniel must have felt when they told the angel, "I am too weak to even speak to you," but the angel gave them the strength to speak and to respond. (See Daniel 10 and Revelation 1.) I can only tell you what I saw in my spirit. I can't tell you that it was tangible, but it was the closest thing that I can imagine to a vision.

As I was prostrate on the floor, it seemed I heard the Lord say, "Look, look!" As He was literally giving me the strength and the courage to look, I saw a heavenly being, and he said three things to me: "That thing that has been coming against you and your family and especially your ministry has an assignment on it to destroy you. It has an assignment to tear up, rip you apart, and annihilate everything that you have built yourself up for. It is bent on totally obliterating you. But what the devil has meant for bad, I, the Lord God, am going to turn it around for your good. Things are about to turn, shift, and change on your behalf today."

In the spirit, I could see that this being was standing up and literally turning himself around right in the middle of my family room and continuing to say, "Today is Turnaround Day. It will never be the same again. Today is Turnaround Day. It will never be the same again." And as soon as he would stop, he would take his finger and turn it around in circles over and over again. I can still see the smile on his face as he was doing this. I can't begin to articulate the joy, the excitement, and the overwhelming wonder that was in that room. I could literally feel my spirit turning around over and over. Then he said, "I want you to get upon your feet and literally turn yourself around three times, in representation of the Father, Son, and the Holy Spirit. Then when you turn around the third time, shout! The victory is in your mouth."

Joshua told the children of Israel, "Shout; for the Lord hath given you the city" (Josh. 6:16). The devil wants to steal our shout. He is trying to stop us from shouting, and if not stop us, then at least quiet us. But it's time to lift our voice like a trumpet. David said, "Shout unto God with a voice of triumph" (Ps. 47:1). The enemy knows that if we open our mouths and begin to shout and praise God, the walls in our lives will come down and that the chains will fall off of our lives and our families. The enemy will have to flee, because he is not going to stand around to hear us worship and praise God.

It was getting to be daybreak, and I was still elated by the presence and glory of God when I was instructed to "go and get Jamie up and share this vision and then follow my instructions." I woke up my husband and tried to share all of the experiences that I had encountered in the past three to four hours. Then the Spirit of God spoke and said, "Now go outside on your front deck and do the same thing that I told you to do in the family room." What had happened *inside* our house was about to be literally broken in the heavenlies *over* our house as we obeyed God outside in the atmosphere.

Now I don't know about where you live, but where we live in our subdivision, at around seven o'clock in the morning everyone is going to work. Here we are in our pajamas and bathrobes on our front deck speaking and declaring at the top of our voices, "In the name of the Father, in the name of the Son, in the name of the Holy Spirit! Hallelujah! Thank You, Jesus! Praise God! It's Turnaround Day!"

It was a sight to behold. Our neighbors were pointing at us; some were looking at us real hard. Others were totally ignoring us, and others were shaking their heads at us. I know what they were thinking: *That is so pitiful, and they have children, too!* Even now I think that our neighbors think that we drive a spaceship. But mind you, we are the first ones that they come to when they need prayer. You talk about feeling crazy! I felt like an idiot, but I didn't care what they said or how they felt, thought, or acted. I needed a miracle, and I had a word from God that this was my "turnaround day." I was determined to follow His instructions down to the nth degree.

We immediately began to see results. My family members began to come to Jesus. My sister-in-law got pregnant after nineteen years of barrenness. The phone began to ring for open doors for the ministry. God opened the floodgates of exposure, and now I am sitting here writing this book with one of the greatest publishers in Christian retailing all because of a word from God and some crazy faith and obedience.

God is waiting on you to get the "you" out of you and for you to step out in a level of faith that may seem crazy to everybody—even to yourself. But are you willing to be a fool for God?

What God showed me through this experience was that He wants my faith and obedience. He wants me to do what He tells me to do, when He tells me to do it, and to do it in faith, because on the other side of my faith and obedience, there is a breakthrough and a miracle.

Getting Out of the Comfort Zone

One of the greatest testimonies I've ever heard took place at a ladies' conference that I took part in. Over twenty-five hundred women had gathered that weekend to hear from God.

I remember one lady in particular who stood out from the crowd. On the surface, everything about her was picture perfect: her hair, makeup, clothes, shoes, and social status as the wife of a prominent doctor. But on the inside, she was distressed in her spirit because her only child, a son, was addicted to crack cocaine. He was married and had a beautiful child, but the marriage was in a lot of trouble because of his drug addiction. This lady and her husband, as parents of this man, sent him literally around the world to get treatment, but to no avail. Things had finally come to a head, and desperate, she came to the meetings at the conference. This was her last chance.

New to the Pentecostal experience, she had just recently been baptized with the power of the Holy Spirit. As the keynote preacher that night, I happened to be preaching on Matthew 11:12: "And from the days of John the Baptist until now the kingdom of heaven suffereth violence, and the violent take it by force." As I was sharing the meaning of exercising violent faith and taking back what is rightfully ours (see chapter four), the power of God began to move, and the Word was going forth mightily. I shared with the ladies how we have the power through the name of Jesus, the blood of Jesus, the power of the Word, and through agreement in prayer to take back from the devil what is ours.

God wants us to live and walk by faith, and what He desires most from us as His children is faith and obedience. God wants us to listen to His voice and do what He says to do the first time, and to do it with joy, with anointing, and with excellence. I love it when my children listen and do what I tell them to do the first time. (It rarely happens. But when it does, it blesses me.) It is the same way with Father God. He wants us balanced, focused, and obedient to His voice every single day of our lives.

I shared with the group of ladies how the Holy Spirit had been dealing with my husband and me about getting out of our comfort zone. Sometimes in order to have what you have never had before, you have to do something you have never done before, because on the other side of your obedience is the miracle you have been waiting and believing for all along.

To reiterate and to drive home my point about faith and obedience, I said something that wasn't in my notes and wasn't even on my mind; it just came up out of my spirit. I said to those ladies, "For instance, if God tells you to sit down on this floor, take your shoes off, and run around this building ten times, then do it. Because on the other side of your faith and your obedience are your breakthrough and miracle."

Bless my soul, if hundreds of women didn't begin to plop down on the floor, take off their shoes, and begin to run around that huge auditorium, barefooted—some with stockings, but all of them shoeless. It was a sight to behold. Not only had faith exploded in that building, but someone had just received a *rhema* word from the Lord.

When the Spirit finally lifted, women were sweating, makeup was smeared, hosiery had runs in them, and hotel personnel who had peeked in to relieve their curiosity wound up saved by the power of God. My, what glory, anointing, and mighty breakthroughs that had invaded our very beings! All of us ended up with our faces on the floor in honor and adoration of what God was obviously doing in our lives. Even in the wee hours of the morning, some of those women were being physically carried back to their rooms, still under the anointing of the Spirit of God.

When the meeting had ended, this prominent lady went home, and as she walked through the door, her husband greeted her. "How was your meeting, dear?" he said.

"Great! You're not going to believe what happened to me!"

"Well," he reluctantly responded, "before you go any farther, let me tell you what has happened. Our son is gone, and no one knows where he is, not even any of his biggest party buddies. His wife has taken the baby and has gone to her mother's house and says she can't take it anymore. She wants a divorce so that she can start a new life for the baby and her. What are we going to do?"

The wife, still very much pumped in faith, said to her husband, "I tell you what I'm going to do. I am going upstairs. I have a word from God, and I have to go and do something I have never done before."

She went upstairs, took her shoes off, put on her Reebok tennis shoes, her jogging outfit, went back downstairs, and said to her husband, "I have an assignment to do; I'll be back."

When God gives you a *rhema* word, you don't need to get some-body else's opinion. Paul said, "When God separated me and called me by His grace, I did not confer with flesh and blood." (See Gala-tians 1:15–16.) You don't need to ask people, "What should I do about this? How would you handle this? What did you do when this happened to you?" *No!* When you have a sure word from the Lord, do what *He* tells you to do right then. Period!

The lady went outside, got into her car, and drove over to her son's house, which was located in a really nice subdivision. She got out of her car, and the first thing she said, with her Bible held up to the heavens, was, "Now, God, *You said,* 'Believe in the Lord Jesus, and you will be saved—*you and your household.*' That boy is a part of my house. As matter of fact, he is the only child I have, and the devil is not going to have him. He belongs to You, God, and he belongs to me. Now, God, I ran around that convention center that night like an idiot because I understand that in order to have what I have never had before, sometimes I have to do what I have never done before. *You said,* 'The kingdom of heaven suffers violence, and *the violent* take it back by force.' *You said* what You desire most out of Your children are faith and obedience. I understand that when I listen to You and hear a word from You, and respond to that word in obedience, on the other side of that word are a breakthrough and a miracle. That's what I need right now—a miracle."

What we keep forgetting is what God said, and promised, in His Word. Sometimes we have to remind ourselves of what God prom-ised us and remind Him of what *He said* in His Word, just as Moses reminded God of His promise to make the Israelites a great nation. (Read Exodus 32:9–14.)

Nobody was at her son's house that day, so she said, "Now I'm going to run around this house and yard just as I did at that conven-tion center. I'm running in faith and in obedience because I believe that on the other side of all of this, there is a miracle."

As she took off running around that house and yard, she said the neighbors came out on the front porch and began to watch her running around this house. One neighbor said to the other, "Girl, is that Dr. So-and-So's wife?"

The other neighbor responded, "It sure does look like her. I wonder what and whom she is running from?"

She related that they looked at her very suspiciously. She said, "I guess they thought I had lost my mind. What they didn't know was that I had lost my mind in order to find it. I knew that in the spirit realm I was fighting for my son's life and this may be my last opportunity to win him back. I was willing to do anything to see victory come, even to the extent of letting my mind be controlled by what I knew was the Holy Spirit's leading."

You see, it doesn't matter how humble or how crazy a word may be if God tells you to do something, then do it. Listen to the exhortation of Paul: "Don't copy the behavior and customs of this world, but let God transform you into a new person by *changing the way you think*. Then you will know what God wants you to do, and you will know how good and pleasing and perfect his will really is" (Rom. 12:2, NLT). He said, "Do not be proud, but accept humble duties" (Rom. 12:16, GNT).

What the world sees as foolish, God sees as obedience to Him. He told us, "It is given unto you to know the mysteries of the kingdom of heaven" (Matt. 13:11). The disciples asked Jesus, "'Who is the greatest in the kingdom of heaven?' He called a little child and had him stand among them. And he said: 'I tell you the truth, unless you change and become like little children, you will never enter the kingdom of heaven.' Therefore, whoever humbles himself like this child is the greatest in the kingdom of heaven'" (Matt. 18:1–4, NIV). Little children have no pretentious worries about anything. They are carefree to do and be who their Father created them to be.

It doesn't matter what people say about you or what they may think of you. The only thing you know is that the Father has spoken to you and given you a word for your miracle and breakthrough. One word from God can change everything. So therefore you move in faith and obedience, and then you watch God. It may seem like crazy faith, but I need to ask you a question: how bad do you want your miracle? Paul said, "The natural man receiveth not the things of the Spirit of God: for they are foolishness unto him: neither can he know them, because they are spiritually discerned" (1 Cor. 2:14). Your family may think that you are crazy. Your children may think that you are crazy, but what really matters is what God thinks and what you are believing for.

Gideon thought it was crazy when God told him to send 21,700 soldiers home and fight the entire Midianite army with just 300 men. In the natural it looked and sounded ridiculous, and would seem suicidal, but God wanted to get glory for what the devil thought would be sure defeat. (Read Judges 7.)

So this prim-and-proper lady did something totally crazy. She said she ran around her son's house, speaking in tongues, declaring the Word of the Lord over him, and declaring his soul for God. Then she heard the Holy Spirit say, "Now go home and get your husband to agree with you for total restoration."

She went home and began describing to her husband the events from the conference and the word of the Lord that came to her. They began to pray the prayer of agreement that they were going to hear from their son and that he would come home. As they retired that night with peace in their hearts, they were awakened at around midnight with a phone call.

She picked the phone up and very calmly said, "Hello?"

On the other end of the line a very frantic voice said, "Mom, have you been at my house today?"

"Yes, son," she responded. "I have been at your house praying and believing for a miracle in your life and family."

He said, "I knew it! I walked through the door tonight and something knocked me to my knees. Are you and Dad still up? My life is a mess. I need for you guys to pray with me. Can I come over right now? I know it's late, but I'm desperate."

He came over that night, and God gloriously saved him and set him free. Sometimes in order to have what you have never had before, you have to do what you have never done before. I'm sure all the laughing and snickering from the neighbors was worth it to that mama to see her son break through to total victory.

LOSE YOUR MIND

Now my question to you is this: how far are you willing to go to walk out in crazy faith and blinding obedience? Will you be like Peter and say, "Lord, if it's you...tell me to come to you on the water" (Matt. 14:28, NIV)? Or will you be like Thomas and say, "Except I shall *see* in his hands the print of the nails, and put my finger into the print of the nails, and thrust my hand into his side, I will not believe" (John 20:25, emphasis added).

Paul summed up crazy faith best when he told the Corinthians:

> Stop fooling yourselves. If you count yourself above average in intelligence, as judged by this world's standards, you had better put this all aside and be a fool rather than let it hold you back from the true wisdom from above. For the wisdom of this world is foolishness to God. As it says in the book of Job, God uses man's own brilliance to trap him; he stumbles over his own "wisdom" and falls. And again, in the book of Psalms, we are told that the Lord knows full well how the human mind reasons and how foolish and futile it is. So don't be proud of following the wise men of this world. For God has already given you everything you need. He has given you Paul and Apollos and Peter as your helpers. He has given you the whole world to use, and life and even death are your servants. He has given you all of the present and all of the future. All are yours, and you belong to Christ, and Christ is God's.
>
> —1 CORINTHIANS 3:18–23, TLB

I believe that, right now, you are breaking through into victory as the Holy Spirit is leading and directing you to your God-ordained destiny. David said, "Teach me to do Your will, for You are my God;

let Your good Spirit lead me into a level country and into the land of uprightness"(Ps. 143:10, AMP). I believe that you are getting ready to lose your mind so that Christ can transform it by His power to see His kingdom come in your life. Paul said, "Do not be conformed to this world, but be transformed by the renewing of your mind, that you may prove what is that good and acceptable and perfect will of God" (Rom. 12:2, NKJV).

I love to go power walking as a form of exercise. What I have learned is that the last lap is the time not to slow down, but a time to press on and push yourself as hard as possible in order to burn the most calories before you end your walk, followed by a cool down. So in essence, I want you to do just that in the spirit realm. Let's press, push, and be determined that you will get your breakthrough and win, because you are willing to press into God. Remember, no pain, no gain!

I count not myself to have apprehended: but this one thing I do, forgetting those things which are behind, and reaching forth unto those things which are before, I *press* toward the mark for the prize of the high calling of God in Christ Jesus.

—PHILIPPIANS 3:13–14, EMPHASIS ADDED

Here is something else I have learned: The fastest runners and the greatest heroes don't always win races and battles.

—ECCLESIASTES 9:11, CEV

Remember that in a race everyone runs, but only one person gets the prize. You also must run in such a way that you will win. All athletes practice strict self-control. They do it to win a prize that will fade away, but we do it for an eternal prize. So I run straight to the goal with *purpose* in every step. I am not like a boxer who misses his punches. I discipline my body like an athlete, training it to do what it should. Otherwise, I fear that after preaching to others I myself might be disqualified.

—1 CORINTHIANS 9:24–27, NLT, EMPHASIS ADDED

Chapter Ten

PRESS, PUSH, AND PURSUE

IMAGINE YOURSELF IN a race, say, the Boston Marathon—the granddaddy race of them all. There you are, under the warm, brilliant sun. Runners waiting for the starting signal surround you. Suddenly the starting gun is fired, and the race begins. As you establish your stride, you begin to sweat, but it doesn't faze you because you have been here before. The aches in your back, thighs, and calves tell you that you are beginning to feel the aging process creep up on you. But even that doesn't deter you. Pain is a part of the route, so you persevere. These little aches and pains are only trophies of your ardent workout and reminders of how sweet the victory will be. You have one goal in mind: don't try and win it in record time, just win.

The miles turn into more aching miles as you think to yourself, *Am I going to make it? Yes I will! I can do this!* You push your body and your legs even harder to get them to go up, go down, get up, go down. Your mind begins to think of the nursery rhyme about the little train that said in syncopation, *I think I can! I think I can!* As you look up from the sweat, feeling the excruciating pain streaking through your body, there it is. It's the finish line—the long, tight winning ribbon. You envision yourself with your hands lifted high, pressing and pushing yourself with every ounce of energy that is left, saying with the little train, "I know I can! I know I can!" You take one gigantic long stride, head first, the ribbon breaks, and the crowd cheers! *Wow! Sweet victory! Whew! I'm tired!*

When you are competing in a race, there are certain guidelines and disciplines that your body has to become accustomed to:

maintaining a proper diet, getting up at the crack of dawn, wearing clothing that is conducive for running, and physical training. Don't forget those infamous warm-ups—stretching, straining, bending, and also training your mind to prepare for the race, as well as checking yourself for mental alertness and stamina to set in mind the goal for that day and having a mind-set to obtain it. As any serious runner knows, "No pain, no gain." There will be some sweating, some knee pain, some calf soreness. Your legs are going to throb and feel as if they can't move another inch, but there is this thing called "drive" that you can't get past. You have always wanted to win, to be on top, and you know as a runner, it is going to take a lot of focus in pursuing the prize.

It is the same in the spirit realm. Paul said, "I discipline my body like an athlete, training it to do what it should" (1 Cor. 9:27, NLT). There are some disciplines to winning this race and to getting the prize: effectual fervent prayer, fasting, studying the Word of God, and communing with other believers in God's house. Sometimes it will mean getting up early in the morning before everybody else does and tarrying before the Lord in passionate prayer, buffeting that flesh and telling it to operate and cooperate with the Spirit of God to see the kingdom of God established in your situation.

The Movers and the Shakers

It has always been human nature to press, push, and pursue; we want to win and win big. We refer to people who are privy to the latest and the greatest in society as "the movers and the shakers." They are much like the men of Issachar, "which were men that had understanding of the times" in their day (1 Chron. 12:32).

At every stage in life we are encouraged and driven to go after our goals and dreams with gusto. As children we role-played becoming someone rich, famous, brave, or all of these. Then in our teenage and young adult years we aggressively pursued our goals for the future. And as adults, most times our success is based on what we've achieved in life. We are always in pursuit of something. Sometimes we fail to enjoy all of the blessings we do have, because we're too busy coveting what somebody down the street has.

Many of us are perfectionists at heart. That's why:

- The house has to be clean.
- The yard has to be mowed just so.
- The pair of shoes has to match our dress perfectly.
- We have to wear the right tie with the right suit.

Everything has to be in order and perfect (within reason) to feel totally fulfilled. God put it in us to achieve our goals. It is drive within us that makes us change a diaper and answer the telephone and a question, all at the same time.

Consequently, that is the reason for the long twelve-hour days, pushing ourselves to make one more sale, even if it means missing a son's baseball game or a daughter's piano recital. But as women, there is also another part of us that will go to any length to take care of what is truly important. That's why when a judge, a court-appointed attorney, or even a father gives up on that son, it is that mother who will go out and sell her blood, if she has to, to bail him out of jail. Women are the pressers, the pushers, and the pursuers, and according to what our passion and drive is, we will get the job done, regardless!

Even at the young ages of eight and five, our two daughters are constantly pursuing our attention, approval, and affirmation and constantly fighting to be the one to achieve that attention first—a look, a nod, a smile, anything that says, "I affirm you. I approve you." Even at school from their peers, they are trying to gain acceptance and approval in their little cliques. Think of the young girl who is pursuing cheerleading, or the young guy wanting to be the next star quarterback on his football team. It is a mind-set to gain acceptance or an approval rating toward something—pressing and pushing for relationships, acceptance, recognition, and status.

Even as you read this book, there is something in your heart, mind, and spirit for which you are believing God. In fact, the very title of this book is why some of you have it in your hands. Your curiosity got the best of you. Just by having it in your possession, you are already in hot pursuit of going further and deeper in your faith, because you know at the end of your violent, pressing, pushing, and pursuing faith, there is a prize. What is that prize? It may be a baby, a renewal, a restoration, a breakthrough, or a divine intervention.

BIRTHING A DREAM

I believe that God has placed this book in your hands to birth whatever He has put in your spirit. What many of you don't know and realize is that you have no choice but to birth this thing. There is no turning back; it's too late. God has rudely awakened you out of your slumber, and you've joined ranks with this forcefully marching army. You've come too far in your knowledge of what God expects, because "to whom much is given, from him much will be required" (Luke 12:48, NKJV). Maybe it's a ministry that the Father needs. He needs your mouth, your feet, your hands, and your arms.

Paul wrote to the Philippian church and said, "Brethren, I count not myself to have apprehended [or I'm still not all that I should be and want to be]: but this one thing I do, forgetting those things which are behind..." (Phil. 3:13).

What are the things that are behind you, or even better, what is it that you need to put behind you?

- The abuse
- The lies
- The bankruptcy
- A failed marriage
- Failure in raising children
- Financial mistakes
- The abortion
- The adultery
- Gaining or losing weight

Paul offers the answer, "Reaching forth unto those things *which are before*" (Phil. 3:13, emphasis added).

We need to stop reaching back and start reaching forth. How often do we find ourselves dragging up the past, rehearsing it, rewinding it in our minds, and playing it over and over again? But Paul said, "Forget it."

Instead of reaching back, reach forth toward the miracles, the restoration, the financial breakthroughs, and the divine purpose in God. Talk to yourself, and encourage yourself in the Lord. David did it when he was confronted with the Amalekites stealing his wives, children, and everything else that belonged to him and his men. The Bible says, "David was greatly distressed; for the people spake of stoning him, because the soul of all the people was grieved, every man for his sons and daughters: but David encouraged himself in the Lord his God" (1 Sam. 30:6).

Sometimes there's no one else around to encourage you but you. It is you who have to pick yourself up off that floor and tell yourself, *Oh, I know I blew it! That thing was meant to take me out and to destroy me. The devil told me that I couldn't make it, but the devil is a liar! I'm going to make it, because "if God be for me, who can be against me . . . I am an overcomer."* (See Romans 8:31; 1 John 2:13.)

If you are a woman who has ever experienced childbirth, and you see the title of this chapter, then you will certainly understand the first two words very well: *press* and *push*. But even if you have never experienced childbirth, you will still understand the meaning of these words.

The thought to press and push is often associated with giving birth. During the birthing process a woman is asked to press and push (or bear down). As the woman begins to experience active labor, contractions (also known as labor pain) help to birth the baby. Childbirth is a process from start to finish that is nothing short of miraculous.

God wants everyone of us to press, push, and pursue Him with all of our hearts and birth those dreams, visions, and prayers that He has placed within us, His children. He wants us to pursue His best for our lives. Until we press and push into Him, the things that have been birthed supernaturally in our spirits will never be born in the natural.

Unless we are willing to go through the labor of "birthing" our dream and get actively involved in doing all that is possible to see it come to pass, we will never see the full manifestation of those things that we have only seen with our spirit eyes. Getting rid of everything that is not like Him and everything that doesn't line up with the Word of God will be the key to seeing that baby cleaned up and handed to you. Your spiritual birth canal, which may seem dark, certainly unknowing, and out of your cozy comfort zone, is the only way out. It is the only way to be born into the purpose of God.

We live in a world that is obsessed with trying to climb the corporate ladder of success. People want to become millionaires overnight and become the very essence of success simply by the car they drive, the clothes they wear, or the house they live in. They set their goals and aim high. And if anyone gets in their way, that person *will* get run over.

There is nothing wrong with setting goals, because King Solomon instructs us, "My child, don't lose sight of planning and insight. Hang on to them, for they fill you with life and bring you honor and respect. They keep you safe on your way and keep your feet from stumbling" (Prov. 3:21–23, NLT).

Setting financial goals are very important, but they should never take the place of your trust in your heavenly Father, who is your real Source. "Where your treasure is, there will your heart be also" (Matt. 6:21). That's why He wants us to trust Him with *every* area of our lives, because He is a Father who cares for His children. He said, "Look at the birds! They don't worry about what to eat—they don't need to sow or reap or store up food—for your heavenly Father feeds them. And you are more valuable to Him than they are" (Matt. 6:26, TLB).

To those who are reading this book and have a passion to *press*, *push*, and *pursue* the glory and presence of God in your life and to see those dreams come into the natural, then these three words take on a new meaning.

If we desire to live a life that brings glory and honor to His name, our passion will be to "finally be all that Christ saved [us] for and wants [us] to be," (Phil 3:12, TLB). The passion to press on, push beyond the pain, and pursue Him will be our one aim in life.

The thought of press, push, and pursue came to my husband and me one night very late while seeking the Lord. As we were about to enter the new year of 2002, God had spoken to me and told me to "press, push, and pursue everything that I have put inside you." God had put big dreams inside of our spirits, and from experience, we knew that God's timing is crucial when it comes to stepping out on the things that He had put within us. We knew that we would never see the plan of God established in our lives and in the lives of those we love unless we were willing to walk in obedience and, if we have to, forsake all for the price of having it all.

God is instructing you now that there is ground that has not yet been covered, people who still haven't heard, lives that are still waiting on you to get finished with your test so that you can have a testimony that will radically change their lives. There is still somebody, somewhere, who is waiting on you to get finished with your mess so that you can have a message that will catapult them to the next level. Paul said, "I strain every muscle, every nerve, and use every ounce of my strength to win this war" (Phil. 3:13, author's paraphrase).

What war is it? It is the war for your family, your body, your future, your ministry, your "life abundantly."

There are people who need to know that drugs are not the answer, suicide is not the answer. They do have purpose. They are anointed and appointed. They need to know that they can birth a ministry. Tell them of the grace of God in your experience.

As a matter of fact, let me tell you my testimony to help you press, push, and pursue what God has put inside of you. You have no idea how many times I've cried myself to sleep or how many times I wanted to give up. Better yet, let me tell you how many times I *did* give up, only to hear the Father say, "When you are weak, then I am strong" (2 Cor. 12:10, author's paraphrase).

There were many times when I sang, preached, and ministered while in pain with a fever, swollen and bleeding tonsils, praying for people to receive a miracle when I needed one myself. Then I would hear the gentle voice of the Holy Spirit say, "I am with you; you are not alone." (See Hebrews 13:5.)

Let me tell you how awkward I felt when I knew people were talking about me, criticizing me, laughing and making fun at me, and the Father would say, "Rejoice that you have been counted worthy." (See Acts 5:41.)

People told me that I would never make it in music ministry. They would say, "Just go back home to North Carolina and be glad God uses you locally." But I would hear the Father say, "Before the foundation of the earth I chose you, and I have ordained you to go to the nations of the earth." (See Jeremiah 1:4–5.) I am making it. I'm still not all I want to be, and won't be until I see Him, then that which is unseen shall be seen. (See 1 Corinthians 13:12.)

Maybe you're wondering, *How did you make it, and how are you still making it, Judy?* I'll tell you how. Having done all to stand, I still stand strong in the faith! (See 1 Corinthians 16:13.) I pressed, pushed, and pursued, and I'm not done either. So I continue to press, push, and pursue.

The fact that you have this book in your hands reveals that your life does in fact depend upon how willing you are to press, push, and pursue the things that God said belonged to you. Your spouse, your children, your grandchildren, your dreams, your destiny, and everything that belongs to you depend upon how willing you are to break and shake yourself loose from those things that entangle you and to go after your stuff with violent force.

LAURA'S PRESSING

I have a beautiful niece, who has practically loved Jesus all of her life. Laura has always been a faithful tither and giver. When she and her husband were married, they were very involved in their local church directing the children's ministry and helping in any way they could.

One Sunday, during the offering time, she and her husband had planted a significant seed for the child they would have someday. She said that God had confirmed to her through His Word that she was going to have children. They were not in a hurry to have children, so they waited until they felt it was the perfect time to start a family. When they learned that they were expecting a child, they were over-joyed, and so was my sister Sylvia, who was excited that she would be adding another grandchild to her already growing list.

As the baby began to grow and develop, we were all devastated to learn that the tests were showing that the baby had major complica-tions. Along with Down's Syndrome, it looked as if there were major organs that were not developing. Despite all of the bleak disturbing news, Laura and Eric remained steadfast in their faith. As she listened to the negative advice the doctors gave her, she refused to budge, and like a rock, her belief that God was going to come through for her was impenetrable.

Along with Laura and her husband, our family pressed in to see a miracle come to pass. Laura's life changed dramatically. The Bible became her source of strength for each day. Worship was her breath that she breathed, and prayer was her life force. She was determined to press on to see the fulfillment of the promises of God. It didn't mat-ter how it looked, how it felt, what the reports were saying, and even what concerned friends were saying in order to prepare her for what looked inevitable; she was going to believe God.

On January 19, 2004, Camille Elizabeth was born, weighing in at over six pounds and twenty-one inches long. She was perfectly healthy and whole because this little mommy pressed into faith, pushed, and pursued what He had said. She got her little precious bundle of joy, and she got her miracle.

PRESS IN AND PRESS ON

Some scholars believe that Lydia was the name of the woman with the issue of blood, one who would later become one of Jesus' followers. When you think about someone pressing, pushing, and pursuing, she immediately comes to mind. She represents many women. She was a person who was familiar with intense financial distress of life and knew what extreme pain physically and emotionally felt like. She was someone under severe pressure, who lived in habitual fear and dread, and she had to live with strong rejection from society. She is what I like to refer to as our Lady of Pressing, Pushing, and Pursuing.

Many of you reading this book right now are in some of the same predicaments. But just as Lydia had a choice, you too have a choice. She could have stayed in her house, thinking about how terrible things were in her life. Had she done so, she would have stayed in her condition. But she made up her mind, and she didn't care what anyone thought. She had one goal, and that was to touch the hem of His garment.

Many of you need to do the same thing she did. Determine in your mind that things don't have to remain the same. This is *not* "just the way it is." God is bigger than that, but there is something that you have to do.

While Jesus was on the road to Jericho, He passed by a blind beggar.

> When Bartimaeus heard that Jesus from Nazareth was nearby, he began to shout out, "Jesus, Son of David, have mercy on me!" "Be quiet!" some of the people yelled at him. But he only shouted louder, "Son of David, have mercy on me!" When Jesus heard him, he stopped and said, "Tell him to come here." So they called the blind man. "Cheer up," they said. "Come on, he's calling you!" Bartimaeus threw aside his coat, jumped up, and came to Jesus. "What do you want me to do for you?" Jesus asked. "Teacher," the blind man said, "I want to see!" And Jesus said to him, "Go your way. Your faith has healed you." And instantly the blind man could see!
>
> —MARK 10:47–52, NLT

The Bible didn't say that Jesus called out for blind Bartimaeus, but rather, blind Bartimaeus shouted out to Jesus. He went after Jesus with aggressive faith. "Jesus, Son of David, have mercy on me!"

We need to lift our voices! We need to pray when we don't feel like praying, fast when we don't feel like fasting, praise when we don't feel like praising, and worship when we don't feel like worshiping.

Just like blind Bartimaeus, Lydia had to go after her miracle. Jesus didn't go up to her door and say, "I was just passing through the neighborhood, and I knew I had to come by and touch you." No! He could have done that, but Jesus will never do for us what we can do ourselves.

Just read the story about the man with the withered hand. Jesus didn't just touch the man and say, "Be whole!" He said to him, "Stretch out your hand." With everyone watching him, the man showed he had extreme faith as he stretched out his hand, and immediately his hand was restored to normal.

There will be times when the Lord will ask you to do something that will stretch your faith. Forget what tradition and religion have put on you, and be determined like this lady and blind Bartimaeus, that today is the day of change. The Bible says that she began to talk to herself, and say, "If I can just touch the hem of His garment, that's all, just the hem of His garment, I know I'll be made whole." (See Mark 5:28.) I believe she said this to herself over and over again. She knew the hem had the tassels and the knots, which represented the promises of God and the law that God gave to Moses. It also spoke of covenant, which God had made with Abraham, Isaac, and Jacob. She knew that if she could just touch that prayer shawl, something was going to happen. She was determined that she would not live one more day as she had lived it in the past twelve years.

As she pushed her way through the crowd, she pressed on and pursued her healing miracle. The Bible says that when she touched Him, she was *immediately* made whole. Jesus asked His disciples, "Who touched me?"

But the disciples were very baffled and said to Him, "Master, look at the crowd around you and you ask, 'Who touched me?'"

"No," He said, "Someone has touched me with faith because virtue has left my body." (See Mark 5:30–31.)

There is a difference between the kind of faith that just brushes up against the promises of God and the kind of faith that aggressively goes after the promise and touches Him. That kind of touch says, "I am desperate." As she touched Him with her going-for-broke faith, God rewarded her. God always honors faith. The Bible says that she came forward and confessed everything, and then Jesus called her something that she never got called, He called her daughter. "Daughter, thy faith hath made thee whole; go in peace"(Mark 5:35).

When Jesus touches your life, He touches you inside and outside. She was instantly brought back into fellowship again and fully restored.

MOVING ON

There has to come a point in your life as it did in the life of the woman with the issue of blood. Just as she did, tell yourself that it's time to move on from that relationship, time to let go of that hurt, time for healing, restoration, and breakthrough. Declare aloud, "I'm going to make it." Whether you realize it or not, God is bringing us to a point and telling us, "It's time." Now is the time to bring forth that ministry, believe for the salvation of a loved one, seek to have an intimate relationship with God, and see His power and anointing. Quit second guessing; *it is time*!

Up to now, for most of you reading this, you have received insight, anointing, information, and impartation. You've been to the conferences, bought all the teaching tapes, the anointing oil, prayer cloths, and the like. But now it's time for you to give birth to that ministry or dream and experience depths that you have never known before.

Think of it like a newborn after the doctor has cut the umbilical cord and cleaned that cute, little bundle of joy and placed it in your arms. That's the prize.

Some of you are getting ready to cut the cord:

- Off debt
- Off negative relationships
- Off your old lifestyle

Always remember there will be opposition to your mission. The devil will tell you, "You can't do it, it's too hard," and you echo it right back to God, "No! Not now, God!" You're begging for somebody to give you anesthesia to numb the pain. This part is no fun, and nobody told you it would hurt this bad. When the pain is the strongest, that is when your prayers should be the most intense.

When we meet with the greatest difficulties, that is the time to stir ourselves up into violent faith. We need to ask ourselves: What does the Word say about this situation? What does the Word say about this relationship? What does the Word say about this sickness? Let the *Word* be your *final authority,* not what the flesh dictates to you. God is going to birth something in you. It's too late for anesthesia! So start pressing, pushing, and pursuing! Your baby is coming!

BE FULLY PERSUADED

We need to tell the forces of darkness that we will press, push, and pursue everything that is ours. The devil is not going to have one single thing that belongs to me, because I am fully persuaded that what I have committed to God, He is surely able to keep. (See Romans 4:21.) I believe you are on your way. God is about to open doors for you that no man can shut and shut some doors that no man can open (Rev. 3:7–8).

I believe that there is an End-Time anointing that is going to hit you as you read this book to carry the glory in whatever area that God has ordained for you. That anointing is going to break the back of the devil over your life, children, family, and ministry.

Some of you have only dreamed about seeing these things come to pass, but I want to tell you, get ready to dream again, because there is power in your dreams.

And this promise is from God himself, who makes the dead live again and speaks of future events with as much certainty as though they were already past.

—Romans 4:17, TLB

Chapter Eleven

THE POWER OF A DREAM

MOST EVERYONE KNOWS the story of Joseph, Jacob's second youngest son. Jacob loved him so much that he gave Joseph a colorful coat, which caused his older brothers to become jealous. Joseph was known as "the dreamer" (Gen. 37:19), but as we learned from Joseph, there was power in his dream. Joseph had powerful, prophetic dreams, but he was immature about when to share them and with whom. The Bible tells us that he told his older brothers about his dream:

> *...and they hated him yet the more.* And he said unto them, Hear, I pray you, this dream which I have dreamed: For, behold, we were binding sheaves in the field, and, lo, my sheaf arose, and also stood upright; and, behold, your sheaves stood round about, and made obeisance to my sheaf. And his brethren said to him, Shalt thou indeed reign over us? or shalt thou indeed have dominion over us? *And they hated him yet the more for his dreams, and for his words. And he dreamed yet another dream,* and told it his brethren, and said, Behold, I have dreamed a dream more; and, behold, the sun and the moon and the eleven stars made obeisance to me. And he told it to his father, and to his brethren: and his father rebuked him, and said unto him, What *is* this dream that thou hast dreamed? Shall I and thy mother and thy brethren indeed come to bow down ourselves to thee to the earth? And his brethren envied him; but his father observed the saying.
>
> —GENESIS 37:5–11, EMPHASIS ADDED

When I read the beginning of this story, I always find myself thinking, *Joseph just talks too much. Maybe he shouldn't be telling everything that he knows. Maybe he should just keep it to himself.*

But haven't we all done that at one time or another? Have you ever had a secret that was a good secret, especially growing up as a kid? You just couldn't keep it to yourself.

God began preparing Joseph to be a mighty, valiant ruler at the age of seventeen. For anyone to become a ruler it takes courage, boldness, self-assurance, confidence, and—it seems in Joseph's case—a little cockiness. Joseph was all of these things, and more, and it was just a little too much for his brothers, who were obviously quite the opposite. The Bible says, "They hated him for his words," so when an opportune time came, they devised a way to get rid of this "dreamer." They sold Joseph into slavery, where he went to live in a foreign land away from his father, his family, and everything that was familiar.

Sometimes to see dreams come to pass, God will take you away from the known and thrust you into the unknown. Read about Abraham's and Jacob's lives, and read about Moses being driven into the desert. (See Genesis 12, 32; Exodus 3.)

Sometimes the greatest revelations that you receive and the greatest miracles that God performs through you happen when you are away from the familiar. Jesus described it this way: "A prophet is not without honor, save in his own country, and in his own house" (Matt. 13:57, NKJV).

As if being sold into slavery by your own flesh and blood wasn't bad enough, the wife of Joseph's boss falsely accused him of making advances toward her. He ends up in prison. Joseph's dreams are about to come into existence. Although those dreams haven't materialized, nevertheless, something is stirring. Even in prison he didn't give up. He kept pressing his way, gaining *favor* with the keeper of the prison, and then pushing his way into interpreting the dreams of the butler and the baker.

Then the Bible says, "And it came to pass at the end of two full years, that Pharaoh dreamed" (Gen. 41:1). At this point it had been eleven years since Joseph was sold into slavery and two full years since being wrongly accused and thrown into prison. How is that for timing! Thirteen years of paying a price just for dreaming. But it was time for God to move in and begin to orchestrate his destiny and purpose.

GET READY FOR YOUR SEASON OF SUDDENLIES

Joseph very articulately described to Pharaoh his dreams down to the minutest detail, and immediately Pharaoh recognized this interpretation to be true. The Bible says, "And the thing was good in the eyes of Pharaoh, and in the eyes of all his servants" (Gen. 41:37). Then, *suddenly*—just like that—come the exaltation and the favor upon his life. Suddenly:

- He was positioned over all the land of Egypt.

- He was given Pharaoh's ring, which meant that he had the authority to transact business in the name of Pharaoh.

- He was clothed with vestures of fine linen that only people of royalty wore.

- A gold chain was placed around his neck that spoke of honor and high rank to people who were rulers.

- He rode in a chariot where people would have to bow down whenever his chariot passed by.

- Pharaoh changed his name and gave him a wife of one of the most influential families in Egypt.

Like Joseph, don't quit believing for those dreams that God has placed within your spirit, because—*suddenly*—you will be elevated from the prison to the palace. God is going to send a "season of suddenlies" in your life. Suddenly:

- That son or daughter is going to come home.

- That doctor's report will change.

- You're going to get an unexpected check in the mail.

- You're going to get a job promotion that will put you in an income bracket you only dreamed of.

- That circumstance is going to change.

- That dream is going to come to pass.

One thing that you will need to come to grips with here is that there will always be opposition to your God-idea dreams. There are *good ideas,* and then there are *God ideas.* A good idea *may* happen, but a God idea *must* happen. The devil hates the latter the most.

Like Joseph, people will hate you for your stand, your dreams, your anointing, your godly character, and your integrity. Just because they hate you or talk about you is no reason to quit dreaming or give up on what God has spoken to you! God has put inside of you greatness, stamina, determination, and the grace to finish what He has started in your life.

When God gets done with your dreams, even you won't recognize them. (See Ephesians 3:20.) People will ask you, "How did that happen to you? Who hooked you up with them? How did you get so far, so fast?" Your reply will be, "I didn't even expect this. He did more than I even dreamed of."

I have been commissioned to tell you in this chapter to *dream*! Dream, ma'am! Dream, sir! Dream, single adult, single parent! Maybe you believe that your dreams have died. But I say to you in the name of Jesus, your dreams are about to come alive again. God is about to take that dream you had when you were a teenager, or when you were in high school or college, and shake it up, wake it up, and resurrect everything that is dead with violent faith!

I know that to be a fact, because God has used dreams to encourage me, to stir me, to warn me, and even to promote me and show me the way.

I HAVE A DREAM

On August 28, 1963, on the steps of the Lincoln Memorial in Washington DC, Dr. Martin Luther King Jr., in his greatest speech, declared, "I have a dream...that one day this nation will rise up and live out the true meaning of its creed: 'We hold these truths to be self-evident: that all men are created equal.'"[1]

Just as Dr. King had a dream, I too have a dream.

I have a dream....

- To see my little girls grow up knowing that they are valued, anointed, appointed, and made in the image of God.

- To see people fulfill their potential, regardless of race, color, or gender.

- That the people of God will not be bound by traditions hindering them from fulfilling lives and from obeying the call of God on their lives.

- To see every sick body healed and to see the body of Christ walking in health, wholeness, and prosperity.

- To see revival and reformation come that will bring a sweeping of souls that will be unprecedented.

- That the church will catch the jet stream of revival and grab hold of the quickening wind of the Holy Spirit to see the Great Commission come forth.

I had dreams of having a ministry to see people saved, set free, and delivered. I had dreams of doing a live recording, writing a book, organizing a women's conference, and hosting a mentoring institute. All of these were dreams—*big dreams*—but then again, I know that I serve a big God.

To each one of us, there has been given a capacity to dream. Jesus called it faith. Paul said, "God hath dealt to every man the measure of faith" (Rom. 12:3). The Bible speaks of many degrees of faith. It says to some He gave great faith, others were full of faith, and He gave to others little faith and still to others weak faith, but nevertheless, *faith*. (See Matthew 8, 14; Acts 6; Romans 14.) Faith and dreams go hand in hand.

Maybe you feel as if your dreams have died a long time ago, or maybe you feel your dream is not so much dead, but buried, or maybe even asleep. I want this chapter to be a word from the Lord to quicken those dreams back to life again. Paul said:

> And you *hath he quickened*, who were dead in trespasses and sins....But God, who is rich in mercy, for his great love wherewith he loved us, even when we were dead in sins, hath quickened us together with Christ, (by grace ye are saved;) and hath raised us up together, and made *us* sit together in heavenly *places* in Christ Jesus.
> —EPHESIANS 2:1, 4–6, EMPHASIS ADDED

That word *quickened* is a very interesting word. In this context, it means, "to revive, to hasten, to show signs of life." It reminds me of the quickening a woman experiences during pregnancy. When I was pregnant with our first child, I can remember the first time I felt that precious little baby move inside me. This movement is known as "quickening." The joy and excitement that I felt was inexpressible. She was letting Jamie and me know, "Yes, I'm alive inside here. I am active. I'm coming in just a few short months. Your dream is going to be born."

It is time for you to experience a quickening in your spirit and realize you need to take action to see those dreams begin to live again.

Paul said, "Awake, O sleeper, rise up from the dead, and Christ will give you light" (Eph. 5:14, NLT). It is time to revive those dreams and bring light where there has been darkness. Let me ask you a question: what do you do with something that is dead? Some might say, "You bury it." But I say, no, you don't bury it, but in the name of Jesus, *you resurrect it!* God is going to give you the strength to call those dreams that are not, done! I believe that everything dead in your life is about to be resurrected.

But for every dream there is a striking reminder that there will be a price to pay to see those dreams birthed. Dr. King paid with his life, and for some of you, there will be a price to pay. It may be your reputation, your status in the community being known as one of those "faith people," or it may be dying to self—to what you want or desire. Whatever the price, are you willing to go all the way?

MY DREAM

I remember when God spoke to me about what I was suppose to do with my life. God had impressed upon me to go to Lee University in Cleveland, Tennessee, which was ten hours away from my home. I dreamed of singing, ministering, and being used of God to see people saved, healed, set free, and delivered. I didn't know how I was going to pay for it; I just knew I had a word from the Lord. As God began to make a way for me to go, I began to pursue the call upon my life to study music and ministry. I was thrilled to see how when you step out in faith, God provides.

As I was pursuing the call of God upon my life, I received a call that my father was very ill and that I had to go home if I wanted to see him again. I went home to be with my dad, and after a few short months, he went home to be with the Lord. I never regretted my decision, because those were some of the best days that we shared together.

As time passed by, my heart was heavy because the dreams that God had put deep inside of me were unrealized. I was torn between pursuing the call of God upon my life and leaving my mom once again. The first time I went away was really tough on her. Like Joseph, I was the daughter of my mom's old age. She was forty-four years old when I was born, and now I was the only one left at home, because everyone else was married. As everyone in my family was pursuing their own lives, with their children, I was still at home with my mom, involved very heavily in church work. So when it came time to go and pursue this call to study music and ministry, it was a very challenging decision. Now here I was faced with an even tougher dilemma. I found myself back at home again, my father had gone home to be with the Lord, and I felt deep inside that leaving my mom again would be too distressing for her. So I thought, *I'll just stay with her, because I can always go back to school.*

As the weeks turned into months, the burden became heavier and heavier. I found it very hard to handle the restlessness, the discontent, and the weight of knowing that I wasn't walking in God's plan for my life. I began to seek the Lord about all of this, and He led me on a two-week fast. During this time, I was working part time at my home church. I remember as if it were yesterday. I went to the office to take care of some things before the weekend. As I was going about the office I thought to myself, *There's no one here but me. I think I'll have some quiet time with the Lord.* I knelt that day in the office, and I just began to worship. *Suddenly* I was overwhelmed with the presence of God, and I completely lost track of time. I found myself on the floor, lying prostrate with my face down, crying out to God for direction, crying for souls, begging God to use me. As I was lying there, I began to experience what I felt in my spirit was a vision of a sea of people. There were Caucasians, African Americans, Africans, Hispanics, Filipinos, Asians, Native Americans, Russians—people from every tribe and every nation of the earth.

The strange thing about them was that they all had chains around them and they were crying out for help. There were chains around their wrists, feet, necks, and even their whole bodies. They were crying out to me saying, "Please help us. Please help us."

I said to the Lord, "What does this mean?"

He said, "I have called you to go to the nations, and in My name, you will set the captives free!" Then He said to me, "Speak deliverance to them in My name."

So I began to shout at the top of my voice, "Jesus sets you free! Jesus sets you free!"

All at once I saw the chains popping off of their necks, breaking off of their hands, feet, and their bodies, and they began to praise God.

After this vision, I was so overtaken with the presence of God that I was almost incoherent. At that moment, I knew I had a clear word from the Lord, and I had no choice but to continue to pursue the call of God on my life. My next task was trying to get home and, somehow, break the news to my mom with classes beginning in just a few short weeks. I couldn't drive myself home, so someone came and brought me home. As we drove up the driveway, my mom came out running toward the car, speaking in tongues, telling me, "You don't have to say anything to me. God just spoke to me and told me that you have to go back to school. He said that He has called you to the nations of the earth, and that you must go and obey Him. You don't belong to me; you belong to Him. Go, baby, go; go and obey the Lord!"

I did go back to school that next semester, but my heart was torn because I loved my mom so much. After my father's death, it was difficult for me to adjust being away from my family. I was not yet actively involved in ministry, but I went back to school in faith. I kept hearing the Lord say, "I want you to be with Me. Don't worry because you don't have anywhere to minister. You are ministering to Me right now, and that's why I have brought you here to be alone with Me."

I kept fasting, praying, studying, preparing, practicing, and being faithful to sing in chapel services for the students occasionally. I had a dream and a word from the Lord, so I just kept pursuing His presence. The Bible says, "Seek ye first the kingdom of God, and his righteousness; and all these things shall be added unto you" (Matt. 6:33).

As I was faithful to the Father, He began to open the windows of opportunity, and I began to travel extensively with Danny and Debbie Murray and their group from the college. I began to see the dream begin to unfold very subtly. There was a price to pay for that dream: I never got to see my mom alive again. She went home to be with the Lord, and it was a very hard time in my life dealing with the loss, but I kept pressing toward the goal. Now, even after twenty-five years, I am still pressing, pushing, and pursuing the dreams, because the dreams and the visions are still yet for a season. The great thing is that when God helps us to realize one dream, He gives us fresh and new ones to pursue.

POWER TO PROPHESY THE DREAM

Bishop Eddie Long pastors New Birth Missionary Baptist in Atlanta, Georgia, and it is one of my favorite places on the planet to visit. After ministering at one of his conferences, I retreated to my tour bus with my babies. I changed clothes and was relaxing, getting ready for my short trip back home when there was a knock at the door. I asked my girls' caregiver to please see who was at the door. She starts to talk to three or four people standing there at the bus, and she very hurriedly scurries up the steps and says, "Bernice King wants to meet you." I said to her, "Who?"

She said, "Bernice King."

Wanting to be sure of what I heard, I said, "Martin Luther King Jr. Bernice King? His baby daughter, Bernice King?"

Eleanor responded, "Yes, ma'am, it is."

I said to her, "Bring her up. Bring her up. Get the soft drinks, the cookies, anything. Bring her up. Bring her up!"

Of course, I was very excited to be able to meet this mighty woman of God. I just never dreamed that she would be coming up on my bus, maybe hers, but not mine. As she came up, we began to talk and to fellowship. I found her to be a warm, kind, and powerful woman of God.

At the time we were preparing for our very first International

Institute of Mentoring for women, and I had a brochure with me. As we were conversing in the bus, she said to me, "Tell me what God is doing in your life and ministry." Then she noticed the brochure and said, "Tell me about this mentoring institute."

The first words to roll off my tongue were, "Well, you see, I have a dream." As those words came out of my mouth, I suddenly realized to whom I was talking and what I had just said. Here this beautiful woman sits in front of me, her father, one of the most recognizable names on the planet, known for his famous "I Have a Dream" speech.

I responded very quickly, "Well, not like the 'I Have a Dream' your father had, not that kind of dream." As I was fumbling over myself, we began to laugh together, because she realized that I became embarrassed at the thought of using the exact words her father used in the greatest speech of his life.

I began to relate to her how the International Institute of Mentoring came into existence. I began to tell her how I was sitting in my bathtub, having my Calgon moment, when all of a sudden, God began to speak to me. I don't know what it is about bathtubs and showers, but the Lord has spoken some of the most awesome words to my spirit and some incredible revelations have come out of my showers.

When God first spoke into my spirit about mentoring women in this institute I thought, *Lord, how will I be able to do it? With a husband, children, a travel schedule, and everything in-between, how will this work out?*

He said to me, "In My time, you will see the way clearly and you will know when it is time."

So I trusted it to Him.

When the time came, the Lord told me, "Press, push, and pursue this mentoring institute, and start to raise up mighty leaders. Train and equip them to go and wreak havoc on the forces of darkness and to build up the kingdom of God."

My only question was, "Where?" Where would I put them?

Where would it be held? At that moment, we were in a little building for our office and hardly had enough room for our staff, with a limited budget for expansion. Then God spoke to me and said, "The property that Jamie has been looking at and the building that is on the property is yours. They are asking almost a million dollars for the building and the property, but you meet with them and tell them I said $260,000 and that is it!"

Well, talk about having crazy, turnaround faith! It was crazy to go tell these people that the asking price for their building and their frontage property was off almost half a million dollars, but that's what God said, and that is all that mattered. I had a word from the Lord, and that was that. Someone has said, "God said it, I believe it, and that settles it!" No! I say, "God said it, and that settles it, whether I believe it or not!" If He said it, it will surely come to pass.

I got out of the bathtub, arranged a meeting with the real estate agent of this property, and walked through his door. "Hello, sir, my name is Judy Jacobs."

He said, "Oh, I just love that song you sing, 'There's No God Like Ezekiel's God.'"

Well, he didn't quite get the title of the song right ("Days of Elijah—There's No God Like Jehovah"), but that didn't matter, because I was already walking in favor with this man.

I said, "Sir, I understand you have some property and a building for sale on Urbane Road. Is that right?

"Oh yes!" he said. "Nobody has looked at it for seven years."

I said, "Is that right?"

"Well," I said, "I am very interested in that property because God said that building and property are supposed to be mine. I know you're asking $750,000 for it, but God said to tell you that He needs it for $260,000 and that is it." Then I began to share the vision. "You see, sir, we're not buying the property to sell hamburgers and hot dogs. We're not getting it to put a service station on it to sell gas, but we are going to bring people from all across this nation and around the world to train them to be spiritual leaders. We are going to impart into them principles of training and leadership and then commission them to the ends of the earth to spread the gospel of the Lord Jesus Christ."

I wasn't breathing, and I wasn't giving this man a chance to hardly say anything. His eyes were almost as big as golf balls.

Finally he said, "Ma'am, can I say something?"

I said, "Yes, sir, you may."

He said, "Can I tell you that just the building is worth $320,000, and that's not even including the frontage property."

I knew that to be a fact, because I already had a friend of ours, who was the former county inspector, check it out. He said to me, "He's right, Judy; the building is worth $320,000."

I said, "I know, but I have a word from God. God wants to bless us with that building *and* the property for $260,000."

As the real estate agent realized that he was getting nowhere fast, he said to me, "I'll tell you what I'll do. I will set up a meeting between you and the owner. You can talk to him."

At this point I was well aware that this guy wanted to get rid of me. But the great thing was, I didn't want to talk to him in the first place; I wanted to talk to the owner.

We met the owner and began to share with him the vision. Then the owner said to us, "Well, I don't know why I'm about to do what I'm about to do, but I have to do this. The building itself is worth $320,000, but I will let you have it for $260,000, and then as far as the property is concerned, I'll just give you the property and list it as a tax write-off."

It took everything that I had within me not to take off running and really scare this man to death.

I am not a person who believes in getting something for nothing, but I will tell you what I do believe. Jesus said, "What things soever ye desire, when ye pray, *believe* that ye receive them, and *ye shall have them*" (Mark 11:24, emphasis added). I also believe that I am blessed, blessed, blessed! And I serve a God who is able to do exceeding, abundantly, above all that I ask or think according to the *pressing, pushing, and pursuing faith* that is with in me. (See Ephesians 3:20.)

I also believe in these last days that "the wealth of the sinner is laid up for the just" (Prov. 13:22).

Job said:

> You will also decree a thing, and it will be established for you.
> —Job 22:28, nas

When God spoke that word into our spirits, we decreed that the building and the frontage property were ours, and to seal it, we took a team of intercessors, walked that property, and prophesied over it. We spoke to it in the spirit realm and commanded everything and everybody to come in line with the word of the Lord and with the plan of God.

In Ezekiel 37, God sat Ezekiel down in the middle of a valley of dry bones, and then He asked him a question. "Ezekiel, can these bones live again?"

I love Ezekiel's answer. He was very smart to answer like this: "O God, You know!" Then look at what God tells him to do. "Ezekiel, prophesy to these bones and tell these bones, 'O bones, hear the word of the Lord.'"

God is asking you the same question right now. "Can those dead dreams live again? Can that marriage live again? Can those children be saved? Can your body be healed? Can your finances be restored? What do you say? Can they?"

The one thing that has been reiterated throughout this book is to speak the Word of the living God over your situation. The Bible says, "The entrance of thy words giveth light" (Ps. 119:130).

We must speak to those dead marriages and cry out, "Marriage, hear the Word of the Lord. God said, I will restore what the canker worm and the locust have eaten, so I prophesy to you and tell you, marriage, live!" (See Joel 2:25.)

Tell your body, "Body, hear the Word of the Lord: you will not die, but you will live to declare the wonderful works of the Lord. (See Psalm 118:17.) So body, I prophesy to you and command you, body, live!"

Speak to those children and loved ones who are away from the Lord and say, "Children, loved ones, hear the Word of the Lord: come back from the land of the enemy, come back home! I prophesy to you!" (See Jeremiah 31:17.)

Prophesy to those finances and tell them, "Finances, hear the Word of the Lord: I am blessed, in the city and in the country. I am the head and not the tail, above only and not beneath. I am a lender and not a borrower! So I prophesy to my finances. Finances, live!" (See Deuteronomy 7.)

As we prophesied over that property and building, sometimes we had car horns blown at us, we got really strange looks, and people were inquiring of us, "What are you guys doing over there, just walking around?" It didn't matter what people were saying; I was on an assignment to go after my dream.

I know, beyond the shadow of a doubt, that as you read this, you are being set free and, most of all, becoming violent in your faith. As you do, you are going to see God begin to open doors of ministry opportunities for you. The hour is late, and I hear a "all hands on deck" call that is coming from above. Many of you, like me, have been begging God to use you. I have good news: that time has come. There is a move of God that the church is experiencing right now, and you are going to be a part of it. Are you ready?

But of the times and the seasons, brethren, ye have no need that I write unto you. For yourselves know perfectly that the day of the Lord so cometh as a thief in the night. For when they shall say, Peace and safety; then sudden destruction cometh upon them, as travail upon a woman with child; and they shall not escape.

—1 Thessalonians 5:1–3

Chapter Twelve

THE COMING MOVE

As I STATED earlier in chapter four, in every major move of God there has always been a mighty man or woman of God who has stood out as its forerunner. Throughout these very strategic times, we have looked to these powerful men and women of God to lead us, encourage us, and to inspire us to do mighty things in the kingdom of God. We have watched as God has used them to lay hands on the sick and they recover. They have preached the infallible Word of the Lord to see thousands come to know Jesus as their personal Lord and Savior. We have even seen God raise the dead by the hands of these vessels that God anointed.

How many of you reading this book right now have thought, *I wish God would use me like that*. For too long, many saints have looked to the man (or woman) standing behind the pulpit as someone whom God uses, but not them. But I would declare to you today there is one more move of God that we will see before the Lord's return.

God has strategically placed the church where it is right now. It is one of the most critical times and, yet, one of the most amazing times in our lives and in the church. Prophecies are being fulfilled every day as the coming of the Lord draws closer and closer. Get ready for God to use ordinary, everyday people like you and me in this move.

THE SAINTS' MOVEMENT

Found in this powerful passage of Scripture in Matthew's Gospel, Jesus is plainly instructing the disciples of the power and the authority that are coming to the body of Christ.

181

> When Jesus came into the coasts of Caesarea Philippi, he asked his disciples, saying, Whom do men say that I the Son of man am? And they said, Some say that thou art John the Baptist: some, Elias; and others, Jeremias, or one of the prophets. He saith unto them, But whom say ye that I am? And Simon Peter answered and said, Thou art the Christ, the son of the living God. And Jesus answered and said unto him, Blessed art thou Simon Barjona: for flesh and blood hath not revealed it unto thee, but my Father which is in heaven. And I say also unto thee, That thou art Peter, and upon this rock I will build my church; and the gates of Hell shall not prevail against it. And I will give unto thee the keys of the kingdom of heaven: and whatsoever thou shalt bind on earth shall be bound in heaven: and whatsoever thou shalt loose on earth shall be loosed in heaven.
>
> —MATTHEW 16:13–19

This coming move of God will not be for bishops, pastors, or even anyone in any particular position of leadership. This is going to be a saints' movement. Scripture is very clear about how God has ordained for His church to operate her gifts.

I don't believe in this last movement that there will be an anointing only for a special few. I believe this move will be for anyone who is willing to sell out to God in total obedience. It is for anyone who has ever cried out to God saying, "Father, use me. I want to see souls saved; let me be the one to see lives changed!"

I visualize a move where pastors and bishops will primarily serve as overseers to make sure that there is follow-up, that all things operate in excellence, and to hold people accountable to their walk in the Lord. Get ready to see a mighty anointing on ordinary, no-name people, if you will. These will be people whom no one has ever heard of before, people not on TV, award-winning musicians, or best-selling authors. They have been on the other side of the desert just like David and Moses. These are people who have a word from the Lord burning in their hearts and a story to tell. These are people who have been through stuff and want to share their faith with others.

People who are going through divorce need to know that they can make it. Tell them that you have been there. You know how the loneliness feels, and you know Jesus to be the peace speaker.

People who are dealing with trying to get past a drug habit need to know that they don't need another high. They just need to get hooked up with the Most High, because He can, and will, satisfy.

People who are in debt over their heads need to know that He is a Waymaker, and He will make a way where there seems to be no way.

People who are battling sickness and disease need to know that He is still the healer. You are going to lay hands on them, and through the power of God, they shall recover and come back from the land of the enemy.

In this next move of God, we are going to operate in the supernatural, and it will be a way of life for us. In the Book of Acts we read about how the apostles were raising the dead and blinded eyes were seeing. I believe there is going to be a call back to true holiness and repentance; that is, right living, right thinking, and right being.

People who have been asking God to use them are going to be used wherever they go. I envision people going to get their prescriptions filled, and the pharmacy will be a set up for a healing service. Grocery stores will not only be a place for natural food, but also a place for spiritual food.

The workplace will be a place for people to fulfill their God-given gifts, but it will also serve as a place where the saints will be mobilized like a mighty army to strike at the gates of hell at any given moment. People will come and ask us for prayer and direction.

Sharing your faith is not going to be a passive action anymore but an aggressive display of violent faith. In this coming movement, you will have the faith to tell that desperate co-worker, "Let's meet during break, and we are going to destroy the enemy's plan in your life right here, right now, today, in Jesus' name."

It will be the same on the home front. You will receive an anointing straight from God Himself to lay hands on your children, your husband, your father, mother, or neighbor, and they will be set free.

SIGNS OF THE COMING MOVE

God gave me four aspects about this faith movement that He is sending before His return. He said there is coming:

- A greater boldness
- A new authority
- An intensity in the anointing accompanied by a glory of His presence
- An aggressiveness in the spirit realm accompanied by an acceleration to prayer

A greater boldness

The kind of boldness I am referring to is not a normal boldness. It's not cultural, and you can't inherit it from your mother, your grandmother, or your favorite aunt. It is a boldness that comes straight from God. The Bible says, "The wicked flee when no man pursueth: but the righteous are bold as a lion" (Prov. 28:1). The New International Version says it this way:

> The wicked man flees though no one pursues, *but the righteous are as bold as a lion.*
>
> —EMPHASIS ADDED

I declare to you today as you are reading this, there is a boldness that is going to hit you. It is a violent boldness that leaves you with an audaciousness and a confidence in your faith, in your anointing, in your call, and in your God. You are going to say to the devil, "Get off of my husband. Get off of my children. Get out of my body. Leave my community. Get off of my pastor."

Boldly you will walk into the throne room and get up on your Abba Father's lap and ask of Him whatever is on your heart with no reservation, because the Word declares, "Let us therefore come boldly unto the throne of grace, that we may obtain mercy, and find grace to help in time of need" (Heb. 4:16).

184

Deliverance in the aisles

The kind of boldness I am speaking of has already begun to manifest in the lives of believers. I heard a testimony from one of our workers who had been praying for the Lord to use her to see people's lives changed. One afternoon after work she and a friend went to the local Wal-Mart to buy some things for dinner. As she was standing in the aisle trying to decide which brand of spaghetti sauce she wanted to buy, along came a beautiful young lady walking toward her shouting obscenities at her. She thought to herself, *What is this all about? I have never seen this girl in my life.* All at once, the girl was thrown violently to the floor and began to scream, obviously attacked by a demonic spirit.

Becoming aggravated, the worker said, "What! Lord, all I want is some spaghetti sauce!"

Suddenly Wal-Mart personnel appeared, people began to congregate, and God spoke to her and told her, "You've been asking Me to use you, so go and lay hands on her and command those devils to leave in My name."

She responds, "Here? Now? I don't know if I want to pray in Wal-Mart."

By nature this person is very reserved and quiet. But all of a sudden a boldness hit her, and she went over to the personnel and said to them, "Step back. I'm going to pray for this girl. She is OK. She doesn't need an ambulance or a doctor. She just needs prayer."

She prayed right there in Wal-Mart, applied the blood of Jesus, and commanded those demons to flee. The girl went as limp as a puppy. God totally delivered her and the worker led her to the Lord, right there in Wal-Mart!

If there is one lesson to learn, it's this: be careful how you pray. If you're asking the Lord to use you, it may not be on the stage, with a microphone, under brilliant lights with a camera staring at you, or some other seemingly delightful place. It may be at a Wal-Mart aisle. It may be with a street ministry. It may be in the jails or prisons, in the hospitals, in an isolation unit, in a foreign land, or even next door to you. If you want Him to use you, He will. Be ready; it could be in your good ol' neighborhood Wal-Mart.

A new authority

I once heard a powerful testimony of the power and authority of the Lord Jesus about the late John Osteen. He related how he, his family, and the great Lakewood Church were under a tremendous attack. One day he was in his office meditating, praying, and believing God for direction. As he was praying in his study, all of a sudden, the devil showed up right there in his office. He said that, for a split second, fear arose in him. But the moment that the devil showed up, Jesus showed up right there between him and the devil. (Isn't it wonderful how Jesus will always show up?) When he saw this vision of Jesus, he said to Jesus, "Whew! Jesus, I'm so glad to see You. That's right, Jesus, You get that devil. Get him, Jesus!" The strange thing about this vision was that Jesus wasn't walking toward the devil; He was walking toward Pastor Osteen.

John Osteen said to Jesus, "No, he's behind You, Jesus. Get him!"

Jesus paid no attention to Pastor Osteen; He just kept walking toward John Osteen. Finally, Jesus stepped *into* John Osteen's body and said to him, "Now *you* get him in *My name*."

Along with a greater boldness in this next move, there is coming a new authority. The Bible declares:

> The Spirit of God, who raised Jesus from the dead, lives in you. And just as he raised Christ from the dead, he will give life to your mortal body by this same Spirit living within you.
> —ROMANS 8:11, NLT

The same power that raised Jesus from the dead is inside of you. Many of you do not believe it. You believe it is in your favorite evangelist, or your pastor, or some other person, but not in you. But it is in you. Some of you just don't know it *yet*.

There is coming an authority to every believer who will pay the price for it. Jesus said, "Behold, I give unto you power to tread on serpents and scorpions, and over all the power of the enemy" (Luke 10:19).

We have the authority to go to the gates of hell and tell the devil, "I came after my stuff, and through the name of Jesus, the power of the blood, the Word of God, and the prayer of agreement, I will recover it all!" "God...hath highly exalted him, and given him a name which is above every name" (Phil. 2:9). There is no other name greater, mightier, and more powerful than the name of Jesus, and He is the One who lives in you and who is raising you up to see the impossible come to pass.

Intense anointing and God's glorious presence

I believe the past moves will pale in comparison with the move that is going to hit this planet before the return of the Lord. Ever since the incredulous happening of September 11, it seems as if everything has heated up in the natural world. But there is also some good news, and that is, things have heated up in the spirit world as well. The intensity of God's power has increased, miracles are more prevalent, and the body of Christ is uniting in prayer as never before. We are praying, fasting, and seeing more unity than ever before.

Recently I was invited to preach for a women's retreat. When I arrived, I could sense that something powerful was going on in the spirit realm. Obviously, there had been much prayer and fasting for this meeting. I knew that God was going to do some mighty things.

There was such a presence of God that it almost felt tangible. As we are standing around the altar worshiping, God spoke to me and said, "I am about to show up in My glory." If you understand the meaning of *glory*, it literally means, "the heaviness of God's presence." When He spoke that to me, I shared this word with the two hundred plus women who were in the altar by now worshiping.

As we are all up front just lost in His presence, I had my eyes closed, when suddenly I heard a noise to my right. I opened my eyes, and ladies were falling, precisely like dominoes, on the floor, section by section. It was as if some one was in front of them blowing them down in a beautiful succession. It happened all across the front of that church. What astounded me the most was that it all happened in such order and beauty. No one was hurt. No one fell out of the sequence. It was just so powerful. As we are all lying there for what seemed like forty-five minutes, suddenly ladies began to scream, "It's gone! It's gone! I'm healed! Praise God!" There was one lady who was a lawyer that had a tumor on the back of her head the size of a table tennis ball. When she discovered that the tumor was gone, she went totally bonkers. The glory of God and the intensity in that room with the presence of God was so totally overwhelming that we were afraid to even move for quite a while, afraid of what we might see. I don't know if you have ever been in that kind of presence of God before, but if you have, then you know what I mean when I say reverential fear.

You have to believe that God has ordained it for you to have this book, not only in your hand, but in your house, because the glory of God is about to hit your house in a way that you haven't even dreamed possible. Not because of the book, but because of the revelation that is in the book that you are getting. Right now, stop reading and ask God to visit your house with His glory. Tell Him, "Father, send the glory to my house, my family, my children, my apartment, my job, my life. Send it now. I'm ready, I'm still, and I am yielded."

Aggressiveness in the spirit realm and accelerated prayer

When I think about the word *aggressive*, I immediately think of songwriters. They are some of the most aggressive people that I know. Don't get me wrong. I love songwriters. My husband happens to be one. The thing about songwriters is that they will find you wherever you are—in a mall, the grocery store, or even in a bathroom. They obviously have a song that they think will fit the way that you minister. So they pursue! When they find you, they won't just sing a verse and a chorus of this illustrious song they have written, but they will sing *all* verses, along with the choruses. It is sometimes funny to me.

Now all you songwriters don't dislike me for saying that; it's just the truth. Right? Right! (smile)

But what I'm referring to in this chapter has nothing to do with aggressive songwriters. What I'm talking about is the aggressiveness in the spirit realm that you will experience in this next movement. You are going to go after all the things that God said were yours. In this next movement, there will be an incredible move to operate under such an aggressiveness that when you walk in a room, every demon will have to flee. When you confront Satan's minions, they will run in terror saying, "Let's go. It's not worth it. Look who just showed up!"

It will be such a move that cancer will disappear, deaf ears will open up, blinded eyes will see, because you are walking in such a realm that the power of God is present to save, heal, and deliver. It will be such an aggressiveness that is not moved by anything, because you have set your face like flint, and you are bound and determined that this is your time and your season to have all that God said that you could have.

Also, there is coming with this move an acceleration to prayer, where actually in the heavens, prayers, petitions, and requests will be accelerated. To *accelerate* means, "to go faster, to speed up, to increase speed, to pick up the pace, to hasten."

What God showed me about acceleration to prayer had to do with a memory of my mom and grandma. My mom and grandma were mighty women of God. My grandma's name was Grandma Lonnie. Whenever my grandma was filled with the power of the baptism of the Holy Spirit, she spoke in tongues for weeks. My grandpa was so afraid of her that he told her, "You've gone over to that Pentecostal church, and they've put some sort of dust or some sort of spell on you, and you have gone crazy and lost your mind."

The truth of the matter was that she had lost her mind—in Christ—and she wasn't about to find it. She had found an unspeakable joy, power, boldness, authority, and peace that she had never experienced before. My mom was also a very powerful and mighty woman of prayer.

189

God spoke to my heart and said, "The things that your mom and grandma took weeks, months, and even years to pray about and see the manifestation of that prayer, I'm going to answer overnight!"

One of the greatest financial accelerated prayers that I have ever been a part of took place at a ladies' conference several years ago. A lady had come to the meeting, and she and her husband were praying for a financial miracle. She didn't know when it was going to happen, or how it was going to happen, but she knew it was going to happen. Sounds like faith to me!

As I was preaching this message about accelerated prayer, I gave a scripture from Habakkuk 2:2–3:

> Then the LORD said to me, "Write my answer in large, clear letters on a tablet, so that a runner can read it and tell everyone else. But these things I plan won't happen right away. Slowly, steadily, surely, the time approaches when the vision will be fulfilled. If it seems slow, wait patiently, for it will surely take place. It will not be delayed.
>
> —NLT

She and her husband had agreed that they were finished with debt and would be coming out of it so that they could be free to finance the last-day outpouring of God's power in the earth. They were tired of the vicious cycle of the threatening telephone calls, letters, and all of the other effects that comes with being over your head in debt. So they sat down and took into account the amount of debt that they were in, and they began to progressively pay down their bills. As they did this, they kept giving their tithe and offerings. Then they began to plant additional seed, and mark it, to get out of debt.

Before she left for the conference, they had figured out that they needed $25,000 to be completely out of debt. So as I began to share the word from the Lord about being aggressive in the spirit and how God was going to accelerate our prayers, she took hold of that word and began to claim that word as "her word."

As the Spirit of God began to move in the service, ladies were drawn to the altar, and she was one of the first ones up to the altar to worship. While this woman was standing there in worship, she said she felt compelled to thank God for getting them out of the $25,000 debt, so she did. With her hands lifted up, all of a sudden, someone slipped something into her hand. She thought to herself, *It's probably a prayer request or a note from one of the ladies that I brought to the conference, but I'm not going to look at it right now, because I just want to worship with no interruptions.* As she was standing there, she heard the Holy Spirit say, "Look at it!" She thought to herself, *OK. But I know what it is.* She put her arms down and looked at the piece of paper. It was not a prayer request or a note—it was a check! But not just a plain ol' check. It was a check in the amount of $25,000!

Now let me ask you a question, if I may. What is the likelihood of you going to the normal weekend getaway-in-the-Holy-Ghost conference and having somebody come up to you and give you a check for $25,000, which just *happens* to be the exact amount you owe in debt? Except God! Except prayer! Except accelerated prayer! Like the children of Israel, we are getting ready to get out of Egypt, and we are not going empty-handed. (See Exodus 12:35–36.) Get ready for your prayers to be accelerated as you become aggressive in prayer and in faith.

GOD SAID, "RUN!"

Another lady who attended our women's conference shared a beautiful testimony with me. She came to the conference with her head down, doubled-over, with no self-esteem left, and told the Lord, "I'm going to give You one last chance." All of her life, she had been told she was nothing and wasn't worth anything. She had been abused physically, verbally, and mentally. She came to the meetings with friends from her home church, and she was desperate.

She was taking all of this in as I spoke about boldness, authority, intensity in the anointing, the glory of God's presence filling your house, and aggressiveness in the spirit realm accompanied by an acceleration to prayer. She later told me, "Judy, I couldn't relate to any of these things. They were all foreign to me. I didn't even feel comfortable raising my hands in church. But as you made a point that sometimes in order to have what we have never had before, we have to do what you have never done before, that really hit home with me." She continued, "At one point you were talking about a couple believing for their son to be free from drugs and how she and the other women in this particular conference ran around the building. As you were sharing this, all of a sudden, everyone in the service started running also." (See chapter nine.) She said to me, "When I saw all of those ladies running as a response to that testimony, I became a little uncomfortable. All at once I felt something deep inside me scream, 'Run!'" She thought to herself, *I won't get out there with the rest of them. I'll just run around over here in this corner a little bit to the side, because in order for me to have what I have never had before, I must do what I have never done before.*

She moved a little to the left and then a little to the right, until she found herself going further and further away from the corner. Before she knew it, she was running, leaping, dancing, and rejoicing all over the building, and in the process, God baptized her with the power of the Holy Spirit.

She said, "As I was running. I could feel the chains breaking off, the burden being lifted, and the depression and oppression destroyed in my life, and I knew for the first time in my life, I was free." She just knew when she got back home everything was going to be just fine.

As she stepped into her house the next day, her husband greeted her at the door with a beer bottle in his hand saying, "Where have you been? I didn't tell you that you could leave! You're going to pay for this!"

She said, "As he was standing there screaming obscenities in my face, my head and back began to bow and I began to brace myself, because I knew what was next."

While this is going on, suddenly she had a vision. She found herself back in the hotel conference room. But this time, she was sitting on the front row, and there was no one there but she and me. I'm preaching this message straight to her about boldness, authority, aggressiveness, and accelerated prayer. Then the scene changes, and she sees herself running around the building. As she's running, she suddenly realizes that she was no longer running, but now she was flying in her vision.

Suddenly she comes back to reality, and something begins to happen to her. Authority and boldness rise in her. Something comes up the back of her legs, and her back straightens up. Her head shot up. She lifted her voice and shouted at her husband, "This junk has to stop!"

Her husband looked at her and said, "What did you say to me?"

She thought to herself, *O God, what did I say to him? What do I do now, Holy Ghost?*

She heard the Holy Spirit say, "Get out of the house into your front yard and run just like you did at that conference."

She walked past her husband, who by this time was stunned that she has stood up to him. She walked outside and then began to run around her front yard, just as she did at the conference, all the while praying, "Go ahead, get him, God! This thing is working in me. This boldness and authority are working, so do Your work, Lord! I thank You that acceleration is coming to my prayers."

After a few minutes, her husband came out on the front porch shouting and cursing at her, "What are you doing? Get inside this house."

She paid no attention, but just kept right on running and praying in the spirit, and believing for a miracle to happen in the middle of this chaos.

As she was running, neighbors began to come out of their houses to see all the commotion. One neighbor later confided in her, "I saw you running around in the yard, and I thought, *He sure enough is trying to kill her now!*"

She didn't care what any of them thought. She had a word from

193

the Lord, and she needed a miracle. (You can't worry what people think about you. You have to do what God tells you to do.) As her husband was shouting to her, telling her to get back into the house, the Holy Spirit gave her an idea.

Suddenly she stopped running, and she looked over at her husband standing on the front porch. Slowly she began to walk toward him. She told me, "Judy, everything stood still. The traffic stopped. The birds stopped singing. The earth stopped revolving. Everybody was looking at us. I was looking at him, and he was looking at me. I'm looking at him, and he is looking at me." Then she walked right up to him on the porch, grabbed him by the face, and kissed him right on the mouth!

He took several steps back and said, "What in the world has come over you?"

She thought to herself, *I don't know, because I sure didn't want to do that!*

The Holy Spirit said, "Get back in the house." She got back in the house and went upstairs to her bedroom. Her house was a total mess. She said, "I knew he did stuff on purpose. So I got my vacuum cleaner out, and I started vacuuming. And as I vacuumed, I didn't quit praying, 'Get him, Holy Ghost! Get him! This is really working!'"

As she was vacuuming, her husband came up the stairs and motioned for her to cut the vacuum cleaner off. When she did, he said to her in an I can't-believe-I-am-saying-this voice, "I don't guess you brought any of those cassettes home with you from that meeting, did you?"

She said, "I almost fainted! I couldn't believe how quickly God was working." She said to him as calmly as she could, "Why yes, I sure did. You stay here. I'll go get them and be right back."

She walked so sweetly out of the room. As soon as she walked out, she ran as fast as she could, found those tapes, and ran back. And as soon as she got to the room, she walked in so nicely. (Whatever you do, do it in style, and just be cool! [Smile!]) She handed those cassettes to her husband and remarked, "Here. These are the best ones." He then left the room to go downstairs to listen.

As soon as he left, she got her vacuum again. She said, "I had vacuumed that floor fourteen times, but I didn't care. I started praying again. 'Holy Ghost, finish him off! Finish him off!'"

Then the Holy Spirit said, "Go check on him."

As she started tip-toeing down the stairs, she said, "You could hear the praise and worship music blaring from downstairs." When she got to the bottom of the stairs, her husband was there on his knees with his hands lifted in the air and tears rolling down his face.

She said, "He didn't get up and walk toward me. He crawled toward me, wrapped his arms around my legs, looked up into my face, and said, 'Honey, can you ever forgive me? I have treated you horribly. Will you please pray for me? I want Jesus in my life.'"

She said, "For the first time in our married life, we prayed together, and I led my husband to the Lord. That next week our church started a revival. He went every single night. One night, God gloriously baptized him in the Holy Spirit." She continued, "Now he is a fanatic for God. I can't keep him out of church."

After so much suffering, pain, and heartache, this woman found joy in her violent faith. While everyone around her was telling her to give up, she looked ahead in faith and saw that mountain move.

The same power to deliver and to set this woman's life free, along with her husband and her marriage, is available to you also. Are you ready to receive and operate in a greater boldness, to walk in an authority that will cause hell to tremble? Are you ready to become so aggressive in the spirit realm that the things that you have dreamed of and the things that the Word said are yours are actually brought into the tangible? Are you ready to see the glory of God manifested not only in your life but also in the lives of your children and your children's children? Are you ready to see those prayers answered with acceleration? If so, believe right now that God is moving on your behalf as you move with Him.

Do you have the faith? I think you do! After coming this far, you can expect it to happen, if you will just believe. Get ready to experience that same joy, because "weeping may endure for a night but joy comes in the morning."

Keep your eyes on Jesus, our leader and instructor. He was willing to die a shameful death on the cross because of the joy he knew would be his afterwards; and now he sits in the place of honor by the throne of God.

—HEBREWS 12:2, TLB

Weeping may endure for a night, but joy *cometh* in the morning.

—PSALM 30:5, EMPHASIS ADDED

I will bless the Lord at all times: his praise *shall continually be* in my mouth.

—PSALM 34:1, EMPHASIS ADDED

Chapter Thirteen

EXPERIENCING THE JOY OF VIOLENT FAITH

I CAN'T EVER REMEMBER when music was *not* a part of my life. I recall so vividly as a twelve-year-old kid, traveling and singing with my sisters on an old diesel bus all over the country. It was the joy of my heart. Music is what motivated me and kept me going and got me through my junior high, adolescent, and those sometimes confusing and not-so-pleasant teenage years.

Having grown up on a farm, weekdays were filled with school and farm chores and not to forget Wednesday night church and revival meetings, at least four or five times a year. But the time that I looked forward to the most would be the weekends. While many teenagers were involved in some sort of sports activity (not that there is anything wrong with sports) or being involved with the wrong group of people, my sisters and I were singing on church stages, revivals, and camp meetings all over the nation. That was life as we knew it.

However, it didn't take long on my journey to becoming intimately acquainted with the Father for me to realize that it just wasn't going to be music in itself that would get me through this thing called life. God began to teach me the importance of learning how to become a praiser and a worshiper in the midst of life, and learning how to walk by my faith and not my mama's or sisters' faith. I learned very quickly that worship wasn't something that I did; it was the personification of what I am.

THE UNSEEN JOY

I have always had a desire for the things of God. Even from my earliest remembrance, there has been this overwhelming desire to please the Lord and to walk in a passionate pursuit of His presence. I can certainly attest to the fact that there have been occasions that were not so joyful, although there has always been joy along this journey. There have been many times when I had to offer a sacrifice of praise. There had to be some choices that would be made that would simply say, "I'm going to get on an airplane or bus and go and minister today. I don't feel like it—I'm tired, sick, (or in many circumstances) my babies are sick—but I know I have a call on my life to go."

I would go in faith knowing that as I went, the Father God was going before me to prepare the hearts of His people and that lives would be changed. Deep down in my gut, I knew that if I looked after His "stuff," He would look after my "stuff," and beyond any doubt, I could certainly trust Him with my life.

As I went, there was a satisfaction in going, because I knew that there would be people who would come to know the Lord, bodies would be healed, lives restored. Therefore, it was my honor and privilege to represent the Father and to do it with joy.

The writer of Hebrews 12:2 wrote about the joy that Jesus had as He completed His assignment on earth in total obedience to the Father.

> Keep your eyes on Jesus, our leader and instructor. He was willing to die a shameful death on the cross because of the joy He knew would be His afterwards; and now He sits in the place of honor by the throne of God.
>
> —TLB

What was the "joy" that He knew would be His after the cross?

1. He knew the justice that would come to the Father God because of the iniquitous acts that Lucifer (His ex-worship leader) had dealt to Him since his fall from heaven. He knew

once and for all Satan would be a defeated foe and that He would be victorious over death, hell, and the grave.

2. He knew that He would be the mediator between God and man, once again uniting and restoring man back to his original intent with the Father.

3. He understood that His death, burial, and resurrection would seal, once and forevermore, the redemptive grace to all of humanity, and that the veil would be rent from top to bottom allowing free access to the very throne room of the Father, where even the chiefest of sinners could run to and be saved.

4. He understood that He could save all those whom the Father had given Him to be saved. (See John 6:39.)

5. He knew that He would be the firstborn among many brethren and that millions would follow thereafter. (See Romans 8:29.)

This was the joy set before Him.

THE CHOICE IS YOURS

A joy comes along with people who go after God with all of their hearts. People who are violent in their faith and who dare to do the unbelievable simply because they have a "thus saith the Lord" and who walk in obedience to that word have an indescribable peace in the middle of chaos. God gives joy that even family members don't understand. It is a joy and a peace that only comes from an assurance in God and His Word.

Everything that the Lord demands of you He supplies to you. The Word declares, "To them that have no might he increaseth strength" (Isa. 40:29). There have been many times when I have gotten up on a stage with a very high fever, an infected throat, and a headache that seemed as if my head was going to explode. Yet, there was a determination to do what God called me to do, regardless of how I felt. It was then that a strength that seemed to come from out of nowhere would rise up in my spirit, and I would be touched by His healing hand. As a result, somebody's life was dramatically transformed, souls were saved, and miracles happened. God will never guide you where He doesn't provide. He will equip you to do everything that He has called you to do.

What I have come to realize is that *it is always a choice*. When we decide to follow the Lord in the way that He is leading, and it seems as if the situation is insurmountable, it is then that we realize that it is not by might or by power, but by His Spirit. It is always first a choice—a choice to say, "I am going to follow the leading of the Holy Spirit, and this is going to be a good day filled with God, praise, and worship, followed by destiny, purpose, anointing, power, and miracles." His presence goes with us, and His joy carries us through.

Happiness depends on our circumstances and environment—things that are going on, on the outside—but joy has nothing to do with either one of those. Joy is a fruit of the Spirit that Jesus promised to believers, and it is what we are made up of—on the inside—and it is a part of our inheritance as children of God.

Happiness says, "I have money in my pocket, and nothing could be finer." Joy says, "I don't have a nickel to my name, but I am still blessed, because I have Jesus, and He is supplying all of my needs according to His riches in glory."

There is a choice to having joy with your violent faith. You choose to say, "I know what the outcome of this thing is going to be, so I am going to lift my head up and rejoice, because right now the Father God is working it all out. In the natural, I can't see it, touch it, or even sense that anything is going on, but I choose to praise and worship the Lord."

That is the reason why Paul and Silas could sing and shout in jail, having been beaten many times over, because their circumstances did not interfere with their joy factor. They could very confidently say, "Do what you want to do with me, 'the joy of the Lord is my strength.'" There was a joy that came along with their violent faith and their confidence in the mighty God that they served.

They were just as confident in their God as the three Hebrew boys who said to King Nebuchadnezzar, "O Nebuchadnezzar, we do not need to defend ourselves before you. If we are thrown into the blazing furnace, the God whom we serve is able to save us. He will rescue us from your power, Your Majesty. *But even if he doesn't,* Your Majesty can be sure that we will never serve your gods or worship the gold statue you have set up" (Dan. 3:16–18, NLT, emphasis added).

As Saul was in hot pursuit of David's life, David chose joy:

I will bless the LORD at all times: his praise shall continually be in my mouth.

—PSALM 34:1

Let everything that hath breath praise the LORD. Praise ye the LORD.

—PSALM 150:6

From the rising of the sun unto the going down of the same the LORD's name is to be praised.

—PSALM 113:3

Weeping may endure for a night, but joy cometh in the morning.

—PSALM 30:5

Paul said to "fight," "press," "wrestle," and "keep the faith," and as you do that as Jesus did, there will be a joy that will accompany you. God will set you in a place of honor just as He did Jesus. People will be looking at you and saying, "Can you believe what God did in her life? That situation was impossible, but God worked it all out for her." All the while you are just smiling with the joy of the Lord on your face. You have to see yourself walking in victory. Paul said, "Be glad for all God is planning for you. Be patient in trouble, and prayerful always" (Rom. 12:12, TLB).

If you can see what you are believing for in the supernatural, then you can believe for it to come forth in the natural. Let it be done according to "the power that worketh in [you]" (Eph. 3:20).

PRAISE AND WORSHIP: YOUR SECRET WEAPON

The only thing that will keep your faith joyful is to keep praise and worship on your lips continually. It is especially important when you begin this violent walk of faith to always keep the Word of God near you. Surround yourself with music that will edify and encourage you. As Jude says, "Building up yourself on your most holy faith, *praying in the Holy Ghost*" (Jude 20, emphasis added). Don't forget to pray in the Spirit, because the Bible teaches us that:

> The Holy Spirit helps us in our distress. For we don't even know what we should pray for, nor how we should pray. But *the Holy Spirit prays for us* with groanings that cannot be expressed in words. And the Father who knows all hearts knows what the Spirit is saying, for the Spirit pleads for us believers in harmony with God's own will.
> —ROMANS 8:26–27, NLT, EMPHASIS ADDED

One thing that we must keep reminding ourselves over and over again is that the devil wants our praise and worship. If he can get your praise and worship, then he has your joy and strength, because the Word declares, "The joy of the LORD is [my] strength" (Neh. 8:10). When you remember what his position, authority, and assignment were in heaven at one time, then you will understand why he hates our praise and worship so much.

He was the very one whom God the Father would call on to bring forth such a mighty melodious atmosphere throughout the portals of heaven, the one who was created to fill all of heaven with music that would exude from his own body. Ezekiel so pointedly describes his position before the fall.

The Lord God says: You were the perfection of wisdom and beauty. You were in Eden, the garden of God; your clothing was bejeweled with every precious stone—ruby, topaz, diamond, chrysolite, onyx, jasper, sapphire, carbuncle, and emerald—all in beautiful settings of finest gold. They were given to you on the day you were created. I appointed you to be the anointed Guardian Angel. You had access to the holy mountain of God. You walked among the stones of fire. [A symbol of the angels.] You were perfect in all you did from the day you were created until that time when wrong was found in you. Your great wealth filled you with internal turmoil, and you sinned. Therefore, I cast you out of the mountain of God like a common sinner. I destroyed you, O Guardian Angel, from the midst of the stones of fire.

—EZEKIEL 28:12–16, TLB

Satan was cast out of heaven and was cast down with an assignment to spend an eternity in hell along with the fallen angels that went with him. So he hates it when we lift our voice and magnify and praise our wonderful God. Do you want to know why he hates your praise and worship? I'll tell you. It's a reminder of what he used to have. He has flashbacks of what he once experienced and the position that he once held. Do you know the joy there is in being in the presence of God? Think of the sheer ecstasy of feeling His incredible peace as it surrounds you. Don't think for a moment that the devil is not reminded of that. I think it is a part of his torment and torture of being separated from the Father forever.

I can tell you frankly that the devil doesn't *necessarily* want your children, your marriage, your finances, or anything else that he has so blatantly stolen, but he does desperately want to rob you of your worship, praise, and joy. He wants to shut your mouth from giving God all the glory that is due His name. He knows that when you worship and praise, something happens in the atmosphere. And simply by lifting your voice to God like a trumpet, you're going to get back your children, your marriage, your finances, and all that he has stolen.

203

David understood the importance of praise and worship. He made some major mistakes before the presence of God was brought back into his life again. One man was killed, and the whole country went through a time of being without the Shekinah power of God in their presence. But as he repented of not following the laws and decrees of the priestly duties of moving the ark, he was allowed once again access to the presence of the Lord. (See 2 Samuel 6.)

As he was bringing the ark of the covenant back into the city of David, the Bible says, "David danced before the Lord with all his might" (2 Sam. 6:14, TLB). But as he was dancing before the Lord, his wife Michal, Saul's daughter, saw him, and the Word says, "She was filled with contempt [or hatred] for him" (TLB). It didn't bother him because he told her, "I was dancing before the Lord who chose me above your father and his family and who appointed me as leader of Israel, the people of the Lord! So I am willing to act like a fool in order to show my joy in the Lord. Yes, and I am willing to look even more foolish than this" (2 Sam. 6:21–22, TLB).

The world will always hate you for your worship and praise. They will tell you it is not politically correct, not very dignified, you look foolish, you are a fanatic, you look ridiculous. But it sure didn't bother David, and it shouldn't bother you. We know something that the world doesn't know, and that is, we are about to get our miracle, and they can watch it happen right before their very eyes.

DWELL IN HIS PRESENCE

People often ask me, "Judy, what is it about my house? It seems as if there is always some sort of chaos going on. Someone is always fussing and arguing. There is no tranquility and peace there. What is the problem?"

The first thing I ask them is, "What are you allowing to come into your house? What kind of music is played? What are you watching or allowing to be watched on your television? What kind of atmosphere are you allowing in your house?" If you want the presence of the Lord in your house, then you have to create an atmosphere in which He will be comfortable. If you want Him to inhabit your house, and more importantly your very being, then you have to allow Him to inhabit you and everything that pertains to who you are and what you are.

David experienced feelings of depression about a hopeless situation, and yet he found the strength praise to God and to hang in there through his faith.

> My God, my God, why hast thou forsaken me? why art thou so far from helping me, and from the words of my roaring? O my God, I cry in the daytime, but thou hearest not; and in the night season, and am not silent. But thou art holy, O thou that *inhabitest* the praises of Israel.
> —PSALM 22:1–3, EMPHASIS ADDED

In the verses 1–2, you can feel David's desperation and hopelessness. He felt completely deserted. How often, when we go through a "valley" experience, do we have those same feelings? We cry out, "God! Where are You? Why did You leave me? Are You listening to me?" What we fail to realize is that when our thoughts are clouded with doubt and our focus is on self, we can't focus on praising Him.

But notice how David's tone of voice—and his attitude—changed one verse later: "But thou art holy, O thou that *inhabitest* the praises of Israel" (v. 3, emphasis added). Some scholars believe that the third verse was not a part of the original text, and they argue that it was added later. The argument is that it was added later because it changes too abruptly, too quickly. In their mind, a person can't be depressed one moment and then the next moment be having a party in the Spirit. So it was probably added years later, or so they say. I disagree!

The word *inhabitest* in Hebrew is *yashab*, which comes from the verb "to dwell, sit, abide, inhabit, remain."[1] In this context of scripture, it means that God "dwells" among men; He "inhabits" them.

He loves it when we praise and worship Him. There is nothing He wants more than to answer us in our time of need. Although it may seem like He is far away, He is not; He "dwells" within us if we could just focus on Him. And when we shift our eyes on Him and begin to open our mouths in praise to our God, He is so pleased to hear praise coming from our lips that, in His time, He will answer.

I believe that David understood that as quickly as you can change your confession of fear, doubt, and unbelief to faith, power, and anointing, God can, and will, change your situation. As quickly as you can move your actions and attitude from depression to praise, God will work it out. As quickly as you can move your confession from what you're going through to what God is speaking to you, He can and will change your situation. God is not a victim of our vocabulary. As quickly as you can say, "He is making a way for me," get ready, for a way is about to be made. He is the Waymaker. He just needs for you to put a smile on your face, set it like a flint, and stand and see the salvation of the Lord.

GOD SAID, "DANCE"

I remember at one point, early in my ministry, I was so depressed and discouraged that I just felt like giving up. It seemed nothing was going right, and God had forsaken me. I found myself facing a tough financial crisis trying to birth this ministry, and to top it all off, I had caught wind of something that was said about me that was totally untrue and unfair. There I was—sobbing, lying on the floor, with my nose in the carpet. Of course, I was complaining to God about how terrible things were in my life and how hard I had been working for Him, all for the "prize" of having someone talk about me. I'm sure you have never been there before. Right? Wrong! We have all been there if we are pressing, pushing, and pursuing.

As I was lying there feeling sorry for myself, I distinctly heard the Lord say, "Get up and dance!"

I thought to myself, *What was that? Where did that come from? That wasn't God, that was the devil trying to make fun of me.*

Then I heard it again. "Get up and dance!"

I said, "Is that You, Lord?"

He said, "Yes, this is Me; get up and dance."

There is a violent faith that has to come to your shout, your dance, your walk, and your talk if you are going to see victory. Sometimes you will be forced to walk your walk instead of talking your talk.

I thought to myself, *How in the world can I shout, dance, and rejoice in the middle of all of this?* So I said to the Lord, "OK, God, all my life I have tried to obey You, and I'm going to do it now, because I *will* to obey Your will."

So as I was lying there, I thought to myself, *I guess I could get up on my knees.* And as I did, I thought, *Well, I might as well just lift my hands,* and as I did that, I remembered thinking, *That feels pretty good.* So I opened my mouth, and I managed to let out a few, "Thank You, Lords" and "I love You, Jesus."

I noticed how uncomfortable I had become on my knees, because normally while I pray, I love to walk. As I stood up on my feet, I noticed that strength came to my whole entire being. I began to walk back and forth a little bit. As I did, the better it felt in that room. Before I knew it, I had both hands raised, and my voice was so loud that my neighbor was wondering what in the world was going on. You have never seen anybody dance, jump, leap, and shout the way that I did. Total victory came, and God turned that whole situation around when I chose to obey Him and dance.

God spoke something to me that was so mighty that I will never forget it. He spoke so lovingly to me and said, "You have overestimated the devil in your life, and you have underestimated the power and the anointing of the Holy Spirit in your life. Don't you remember that I will never put more on you than you are able to bear. The devil is a liar, and what he tells you is the exact opposite of what is really happening. If you'll just give me praise and worship, you will see My glory, and the victory will come."

207

The joy of violent faith is seeing and having your family saved and walking in total surrender to the Lord with you, not only down here on this earth, but in eternity. This life is short and is only a vapor, but eternity is forever. What greater joy is there to the Father than knowing that His children are saved, free, and delivered from the grip of Satan's power.

Second Peter 3:9 says, "The Lord is not slack concerning His promise, as some men count slackness; but is longsuffering to us-ward, not willing that any should perish, but that all should come to repentance."

The heart of the Father God is to see *all* His children free from the bondages of Satan's power.

The joy of violent faith is seeing your body healed, seeing those dreams come to life that once lay dormant and lifeless. The joy of violent faith is trusting and believing that your Father God is in control and that He is Lord, and all things are working together *right now* for your good. You have His promise that He is with you.

So I want to encourage you, and at the same time challenge you, to get up, get moving, get those dancing shoes on, and dance on the devil's head, because He is under your feet. And, by all means, keep standing in faith, and you will experience the breakthrough.

...having done all, to stand. Stand therefore.

—EPHESIANS 6:13–14, NKJV

Chapter Fourteen

TAKE A STAND

I CAME TO THE end of this book and was feeling rather satisfied at what I thought was the end of a great revelation that God had given me. In prayer, I began to commit the book into the hands of the Lord, feeling very content with this accomplishment. I really felt great at marking off this little baby from my "to do" list. But as those who have worked with me on this book can confirm, I began to ponder each chapter (and seemingly every word) as I had done many times over. All at once, a sense of incompleteness overwhelmed me. It suddenly dawned on me that I was not finished with this book.

THE "STANDING STANCE"

I felt at the beginning of this project that it had to be an all-encompassing work, from start to finish, as to what the Holy Spirit wanted to say to the body of Christ. Then I questioned, "What happens if the revelation of this book does 'rudely awaken' everyone who ingests the disclosure of it? What if people do get radical in their faith and follow the steps to violent faith, rise up in their God-given authority, and have joy in the midst of it all, and still *nothing* happens?

I sensed in my spirit someone saying, "But what can I do if *nothing* is working?" So for everyone who feels as if they have done it all, and yet there is no victory—or so it seems—I have written this chapter for *you*. My desire is for you to be able to turn to this book during times of discouragement and to do as Paul the Apostle so pointedly commands—"stand."

I can talk to you about the "standing stance," because I know all about it. I have had to do it. I am still doing it, and I will continue to do it until Jesus comes. The truth of the matter is that everyone who will ever go after God for broke, everyone who dives in and says, "Catch me, God, here I come," will have to become accustomed to the "standing stance." Moses waited forty years; Abraham waited one hundred years; Jesus waited thirty-three years; and you and I will have to wait. Everything will not always happen overnight, and sometimes, God chooses not to answer even in a way that you were expecting, and certainly not in the way you were praying.

MY FAMILY'S "STANDING STANCE"

When this book idea was first dropped into my spirit, our family was facing one of the biggest battles that we had ever had to face in our lives. Our parents' sickness and ultimate deaths were very hard to grasp, but they had lived full lives and were ready to meet the Lord. Now we were facing something that we never anticipated, and frankly, we were very ignorant of how to handle it.

Someone very dear to us had become addicted to crack cocaine. Prior to that, this person was active in the church and a hard worker. We were devastated when we discovered this news.

God had spoken to me the word found in Matthew 11:12, and our family began to stand on the promises of God. We were going to take back what the devil had stolen from us. We began a twenty-four-hour prayer chain that lasted for months. We cried out to God and bombarded the heavens with, "Lord, Your Word declares, 'The kingdom of heaven suffers violence and the violent take it by force.' Devil, we take him back in Jesus' name."

We persevered, cried, prayed, fasted, and "stood on the wall." After what seemed like a thousand forevers, I can truly say that God saved and set him free. We rejoiced, shouted, testified of the miraculous, and then it happened again. He went back on drugs. Now, did

God fail? No! Did prayer fail? Of course, it did not! "Then what happened?" you may ask.

I don't have all the answers, but let me share with you what I do know. I know that God is a God of mercy, love, and forgiveness, but He is also a God who will never force Himself on you. He invites you to come, "ask," "seek," and "knock" (Matt. 7:7), implying that there are some things *you* will have to do, because God will never do anything for you that you can do for yourself. It is always a choice. Joshua invited the people to make a decision: "Who is on the Lord's side?" and he said, "As for me, and my house, we will serve the Lord" (Josh. 24:15). It is always a choice.

Now has God written off this person? Certainly not! He said, "He is not willing that any should perish, but that all should come to repentance." Have we quit praying for him? Most assuredly not! Samuel told Saul, *"God forbid that I should sin against the LORD in ceasing to pray for you"* (1 Sam. 12:23, emphasis added). We know that he is going to be saved and set free, because we have God's Word on it. So we pray, in faith, believing, and having done all, we still stand.

I hear from many of you every week asking me, "Sister Judy, what do I do after I have stood, persevered, prayed, and stood some more?"

What most of you *want* to hear from me is not what Brother Paul says in the Scriptures but what *you* want to hear. What you want me to say is that you did everything possible to make that marriage work, so leave him! Having done all the praying that you think you can possibly do to see that child, loved one, or friend saved, stop praying, and let them burst hell wide open! Having done all the tithing and giving to the poor, you are still in debt, struggling to stay afloat, so stop giving your money away and get all you can, and then sit on the rest!

No! A thousand times *no*! That would be the easy thing to do. What did Paul say? "...having done all, to stand. Stand therefore" (Eph. 6:13–14, NKJV). Keep standing, keep loving, keep praying, keep believing, keep giving, because a harvest is bound to come forth!

213

HINDRANCES TO PRAYER

Sometimes the reason we don't experience a breakthrough is because something is hindering our prayers. There are many key hindrances to unanswered prayers, but let me give you just four of them. Four hindrances to unanswered prayer are:

1. Unbelief
2. Double-mindedness
3. Lack of patience
4. Discouragement

Unbelief

The Bible says that Jesus "did not many mighty works there because of their unbelief" (Matt. 13:58). I believe that there are many times that Jesus wants to do mighty things among us, but because of our unbelief, His hands are tied. You see, doubt says, "It may not happen." Unbelief says, "It will never happen."

There are two kinds of thoughts: a thought to believe and a thought that says, "I don't believe it." A faith that says, "Yes, I believe that this is going to happen," and a faith that says, "That is too hard for God, that is impossible, and that will never happen." You have either one or the other.

But before you let the devil beat you down with condemnation, remember that everyone goes through a stage, or a season, of unbelief. John the Baptist knew that feeling, and it occurred at the lowest point of his life. He was in prison, moments away from getting his head chopped off, when he sent his disciples to ask Jesus, "Are you really the Messiah we've been waiting for, or should we keep looking for someone else?" (Matt. 11:3, NLT). This was the same John who recognized the Messiah and stated to the multitudes that had gathered to see him:

> "Look! There is the Lamb of God who takes away the sin of the
> world! He is the one I was talking about when I said, 'Soon a

man is coming who is far greater than I am, for he existed long before I did.' I didn't know he was the one, but I have been baptizing with water in order to point him out to Israel." Then John said, "I saw the Holy Spirit descending like a dove from heaven and resting upon him. I didn't know he was the one, but when God sent me to baptize with water, he told me, 'When you see the Holy Spirit descending and resting upon someone, he is the one you are looking for. He is the one who baptizes with the Holy Spirit.' I saw this happen to Jesus, so I testify that he is the Son of God."

—JOHN 1:29–34, NLT

Jesus didn't condemn John even with this little turn of unbelief. He said, "Verily I say unto you, Among them that are born of women there hath not risen a greater than John the Baptist" (Matt. 11:11).

Guess what? Jesus will not condemn you either!

He invites you to take authority over that unbelief. How do you do that? You do that with His Word. Remember how He won the victory over the devil? He quoted the Scripture saying, "It is written…" (See Matthew 4.)

Now here is the key to how *you* will win over unbelief:

Casting down imaginations, and every high thing that exalteth itself against the knowledge of God, and *bringing into captivity every thought* to the obedience of Christ.

—2 CORINTHIANS 10:5, EMPHASIS ADDED

If you will fill your thoughts with what the Word says about your situation, then you won't have time to fill your thoughts with unbelief. That may seem simple, but it is the simple truth. Remember that you have the mind of Christ. Paul said:

Strange as it seems, we Christians actually do have within us a portion of the very thoughts and mind of Christ.

—1 CORINTHIANS 2:16, TLB

I would encourage you to get practical about it. Get some sticky notes and start putting them all over your house to remind you of what God says about your situation, and you will see victory come speedily. Keep believing!

Double-mindedness

Double-mindedness is an enemy to the body of Christ that keeps our faith bouncing up and down like a yo-yo. James addressed it like this: "Let not that man think that he shall receive any thing of the Lord. A double minded man is unstable in all his ways" (James 1:7–8).

When you go to the enemy's gate to take back your possessions, you have to be *fully persuaded* that *you will recover all*. You can't be standing in faith one day, talking about what God is doing and is going to do, and then the next minute be crying, bellyaching, and going about pouting, all mad at God. That is a hideous testimony to unbelievers. In a world that is inundated with fear and void of commitment, people need someone to lead them in a direction of faith. The world needs to see stability. David knew this when he prayed:

> Help us, Lord! There is not a good person left; honest people can no longer be found. All of them lie to one another; they deceive each other with flattery.
>
> —PSALMS 12:1–2, GNT

Jesus knew that we would need someone to lead us, so He instructed Paul to tell the people in Corinth, "Follow me as I follow Christ."

David was a very strong leader. While he was on the run for his life trying to get away from Saul, God sent people who were doubtful, double-minded, in debt, discontent, yet loyal to David and needing a leader. When the Amalekites invaded the Israelites, took their wives and children captive, and stole their possessions, David went after them. With the help of an Ethiopian slave he was able to find out their exact hold out. When he got to where their enemies were, he wasn't standing there saying, "I don't know if we should go in or not. I don't think that we can defeat this army. This thing is too big for us!" No, he took his four hundred men, wiped out an entire army with the help of the Lord, and recovered all, along with a huge bounty.

The reason that he was victorious is because he had a sure word from the Lord. The Bible says in 1 Samuel 30, David said to Abiathar the priest:

> "Bring me the ephod!" So Abiathar brought it. Then David asked the LORD, "Should I chase them? Will I catch them?" And the LORD told him, "Yes, go after them. You will surely recover everything that was taken from you!"
>
> —1 SAMUEL 30:7–8, NLT

He was not double-minded. David had a word from God and was fully persuaded, despite all the negative stuff around him.

Be *fully persuaded* that what God said, *He will do*. Don't go back and forth in your confession of faith. "Let your yea be yea; and your nay, nay" (James 5:12). Stand on the Word of God in the face of what seems very doubtful and perhaps unlikely. God *will* surprise you and go beyond the limits of your faith.

Lack of patience

Sometimes we don't see prayers answered because we become impatient. Especially in the world we live in today where everything is instant, we have become accustomed to having it *our* way in *our* time. God's timetable is not our timetable. He is not on our schedule. If we stand, believing in faith for victory, then we need to learn how to be patient.

Let me give you a short lesson on patience. I don't know if you have heard of the "Kernel of Corn" story, but it goes something like this.

A little kernel of corn was in this big sack along with the other little kernels of corn. Then one of the little kernels of corn said, "Did you hear about the farmer?"

"The farmer?" said the other kernels of corn.

"Yeah, the farmer comes and takes you out of this bag, and then he takes you on a trip. When he gets you there, he buries you in a hole in the ground. *Shhhh!* I think I hear him coming."

Sure enough, here comes the farmer. He scoops his big hand in the bag and takes little kernels of corn with him to a field where he buries them in the ground.

When he gets there, the little kernel of corn starts to cry, "Help! Help! It's dark! Is there anybody listening? It's dark! I'm cold! He's killing me! He's killing me! I'm going to die! I'm going to die! He's cruel! He's cruel! The farmer is cruel!" So the little kernel of corn is there crying out day and night, "Help! Somebody help me!"

All of a sudden the little kernel of corn begins to notice something. He thinks to himself, *Something is happening to me. What is that growing on me?* He starts to notice that he is growing and gaining momentum. Then one day, suddenly, he bursts forth from out of the ground into the brilliant sunshine.

"Oh, look! Look at me! I am no longer a kernel, but I am a full-grown stalk. Look at all of these ears of corn everywhere. Look what came out of all of that. The farmer knew what he was doing. He wasn't trying to kill me; he was trying to grow me."

You may find yourself like the little kernel of corn: in a deep, dark hole thinking that you have done everything there is to do. You are crying to God and thinking to yourself, *I'm going to die. It's cold. This valley is too dry. This water is too deep. I'm not going to make it.* But if you let the Farmer (Father God) have His way, I promise you that one day you will look back, thank Him, and say, "Look what the Lord has done!" And you will give Him all the glory.

I think we all understand the need to have our prayers answered *yesterday!* But God doesn't always answer that way. Sometimes He wants to take us *through* some things instead of delivering us *out* of some things.

Let patience have her perfect work, that ye may be perfect and entire, wanting nothing.

—JAMES 1:4

God wants to take us down a path where He is teaching and challenging us to go to levels of mature faith that we never dreamed possible. The writer of Hebrews even brings this blessed virtue alongside the word *faith*:

...who through *faith and patience* inherit the promises.
—HEBREWS 6:12, EMPHASIS ADDED

In essence, if you are going to possess the promises that God said were yours, you are going to learn to develop your faith *and* your patience. For when your faith is tested, then your patience shines through. Paul said:

We can rejoice, too, when we run into problems and trials, for we know that they are good for us—*they help us learn to be patient.* And patience develops strength of character in us and helps us trust God more each time we use it until finally our hope and faith are strong and steady. Then, when that happens, we are able to hold our heads high no matter what happens and know that all is well, for we know how dearly God loves us, and we feel this warm love everywhere within us because God has given us the Holy Spirit to fill our hearts with his love.
—ROMANS 5:3–5, TLB, EMPHASIS ADDED

Discouragement
I will never forget a time in my life when my husband and I were faced with a dilemma concerning our second and last baby. We were excited about this little promise that God had put inside of us, after the statistics said that it would never happen. We were so thrilled when we learned that this little precious bundle was on the way.

Every doctor visit was a joy because according to our doctor, everything was looking great. My levels were great, everything was right on time, and we could hardly wait to see what God was sending us. Then as the time begin to wane away, my doctor noticed that the baby was not getting into proper position to come down the birth canal; she was breeched.

We weren't too concerned in the beginning, because our doctor kept saying, "Oh, don't worry, she will turn." So we kept thinking, *Yeah, it's too early; she'll turn.* Then the time came when we were going to the doctor's office every two weeks, but still no turning. She had the position of an "incomplete or footling breech," which basically meant that she had found a comfortable sitting position where her legs were stretched out below her buttock, and her legs were in place to come out first.

Finally, it came down to every week when we were seeing our doctor, and now it was just a matter of weeks, and still a breeched baby. That is when the overwhelmingness set in.

We prayed, got our family to pray, called every prayer line that we could call, planted seeds, and just believed that I wasn't going to have to go through a C-section surgery. I did everything but stand on my head, which I might have done if I had been able to do so! We tried playing loud music to get her to turn. (I think she liked that part really well!) We put cold compresses on the top of my belly to try to get this little thing uncomfortable, but I about froze to death. Then as the priest and the prophet of our house, Jamie began to speak to my belly and calling her by her full name and commanding her to get in place and position, but still no results.

At night I would lie in my bed and would find myself so perplexed and could not figure out for the life of me why in the world this baby refused to turn and why our prayers were not working. Nothing was working! All the while God gave me a comforting word from His Word:

> And we know that all that happens to us is working for our good if we love God and are fitting into his plans.
>
> —Romans 8:28, TLB

We never doubted but believed that God would do it right before the surgery, including our doctor. So before I was wheeled into the surgery suite to get prepped for surgery, we went in for a scan one more time, and wouldn't you know it, there she was in her little comfortable position as pretty as she could be. Then the surgery began, and in about five minutes, Erica was born on February 22, 2000. I wound up going through the rigmarole of a cesarean section surgery, but we came through with a healthy mommy and a healthy baby.

There were also some things that I will never know about that ordeal.

Maybe I would have had complications during the delivery, or maybe the baby would have experienced problems. I don't have the answers. But one sure thing that the Father taught me was to trust Him completely, because He sees tomorrow the way that we see yesterday.

The process that I went through taught me a lot:

- It taught me to trust God and His sovereignty at a greater level than before.

- I learned to wait on the Lord and be of good courage.

- I learned that sometimes God won't get you *out* of some things, but He will bring you *through* some things with His grace.

- I learned that as the heavens are higher than the earth, so are His ways higher than my ways and His thoughts my thoughts.

Proverbs 20:24 says, "Since the Lord is directing our steps, why try to understand everything that happens along the way" (TLB).

Don't be discouraged about where you are right now; fight the *good* fight of faith. Remember, it is a good fight, because we win. Maybe this is a time when God has you in His showcase so others can see and believe. Many lives will be changed because of your endurance, patience, and unwavering trust in your heavenly Father. He just wants us to trust Him! Relax, take a deep breath, and trust that He is working it all out for you right now.

From My Heart to Yours

Coming from a strong background of prayer and faith from my family, I was constantly mentored into a culture of believing God for the unbelievable and pressing in to the things of God. Even as a child, I was encouraged in the things of God, but unfortunately, for some people, it was the exact opposite.

Perhaps you find it very difficult to relate with my stance and my background because of your background or past. I would say to you that God is a God of new beginnings. You may not have had a godly father or godly mother to bring you up in the nurture and admonition of the Lord, but God has given you many fathers, mothers, sisters, and brothers in Christ, and sometimes that is what the Father has designed for your life. (See Mark 10:29–30.)

Although you may not have come from a background that was solid in the faith such as myself, or perhaps someone you know, God still wants to use you right where you are, in whatever situation you may find yourself in. The things that are coming forth from the body of Christ to bring us into "the oneness of the spirit" are staggering. (See Ephesians 2:18.) There are no more excuses to what God wants us to learn and grasp. For some of you it will mean "the elementary things" as in Isaiah 28:10, and there is nothing wrong with that. The Bible says, "Despise not small beginnings" (Job 8:7). For someone else, it may mean going on to stronger things, such as the meat of the world. (See Hebrews 5:14.) Wherever you may find yourself, start right where you are, because "to every man has been given a measure of faith" (Rom. 12:3). Whatever your measure of faith is, let God use it to bring you into the fulfillment of your purpose and destiny.

NOTES

Introduction

1. Oswald Chambers, *My Utmost for His Highest* (Nashville, TN: Discovery House Publishers, 1992).

Chapter One
A Rude Awakening

1. "Pearl Harbor," Microsoft Encarta Online Encyclopedia 2003, http://encarta.ms.com, 1997-2003 Microsoft Corporation. All rights reserved 1993-2003 Microsoft Corporation.
2. Finis Jennings Dake, *Dake's Annotated Reference Bible* (N.p.: Dake Publishing, 1963), 39.

Chapter Two
A Passive and Desensitized Generation

1. John C. Thomas, "Root Causes of Juvenile Violence, Part 4: Toxic Society" http://www.family.org/pplace/youandteens/a0011367.cfm (accessed March 7, 2001).
2. Lt. Col. Dave Grossman, *On Killing: The Psychological Cost of Learning to Kill in War and Society* (Boston, MA: Little Brown, 1995).
3. Ibid.

Chapter Three
What Is Violent Faith?

1. Arthur L. Farstad and William MacDonald, *The Believer's Bible Commentary* (Nashville, TN: Thomas Nelson Publishers, 1995).

Chapter Four
The Power of Matthew 11:12

1. William MacDonald, *New Testament* (computer file), electronic ed., Logos Library System (Nashville, TN: Thomas Nelson Publishers, 1997).

2. Karen Wheaton, "It Is High Time" (sermon, Press, Push, Pursue Conference, April 2003).

3. Ron McIntosh, *Keep the Flame Burning* (Tulsa, OK: Harrison House Publishing, Inc., 1994), 15.

Chapter Six
Is There Not a Cause?

1. "Too Painful," ABCNews.com, November 11, 2003, http://abcnews .go.com/sections/Primetime/US/Jessica_Lynch_031106-2.html (accessed July 9, 2004).

2. Anne Gimenez, *Marking Your Children for God* (Lake Mary, FL: Charisma House, 1987), 13–14, 18–19.

Chapter Eight
Don't Quit, Prayer Works!

1. Ron Kurtus, www.School-for-Champions.com/speeches/Churchill-Nevergiveup.htm, May 20, 2001.

2. Myles Munroe, *Understanding the Purpose and Power of Prayer* (Springdale, PA: Whitaker House Publishing, 2002), 14.

Chapter Eleven
The Power of a Dream

1. Distribution statement: Accepted as part of the Douglass Archives of American Public Address (http://douglass.speech.nwu.edu) on May 26, 1999. Prepared by D. Oetting (http://nonce.com/oetting). Permission is hereby granted to download, reprint, and/or otherwise redistribute this file, provided this distribution statement is included and appropriate point of origin credit is given to the preparer and Douglass. Martin Luther King Jr. "I Have a Dream" reprinted by arrangement with The Heirs to the Estate of Martin Luther King Jr., c/o Joan Daves Agency as agent for the proprietor. Copyright (c) 1963 by the Estate of Martin Luther King Jr. Copyright renewed 1991 by Coretta Scott King. (Accessed August 30, 2004.)

Chapter Thirteen
Experiencing the Joy of Violent Faith

1. W. E. Vine, et. al., *An Expository of Dictionary of Biblical Words,* (Nashville, TN: Thomas Nelson Publishers, 1984), 105.

Strang Communications, the publisher of both Charisma House and *Charisma* magazine, wants to give you 3 FREE ISSUES of our award-winning magazine.

Since its inception in 1975, *Charisma* magazine has helped thousands of Christians stay connected with what God is doing worldwide.

Within its pages you will discover in-depth reports and the latest news from a Christian perspective, biblical health tips, global events in the body of Christ, personality profiles, and so much more. Join the family of *Charisma* readers who enjoy feeding their spirit each month with miracle-filled testimonies and inspiring articles that bring clarity, provoke prayer, and demand answers.

To claim your **3 free issues** of *Charisma,* send your name and address to: Charisma 3 Free Issue Offer, 600 Rinehart Road, Lake Mary, FL 32746. Or you may call 1-800-829-3346 and ask for Offer # 93FREE. This offer is only valid in the USA.

---

www.charismamag.com